set
the page
on
fire

set
the page
on
fire

SECRETS OF
SUCCESSFUL WRITERS

steve o'keefe

New World Library
Novato, California

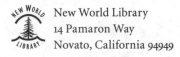

New World Library
14 Pamaron Way
Novato, California 94949

Text design by Tona Pearce Myers and Megan Colman

Library of Congress Cataloging-in-Publication data is available.

First printing, June 2019
ISBN 978-1-60868-611-7
Ebook ISBN 978-1-60868-612-4
Printed in Canada on 100% postconsumer-waste recycled paper

New World Library is proud to be a Gold Certified Environmentally Responsible Publisher. Publisher certification awarded by Green Press Initiative.

10   9   8   7   6   5   4   3   2   1

Dedicated to
Brian Thomas O'Keefe,
who provided most of the words used here —
thanks for the loan!
&
RoseAnn O'Keefe
for teaching me how to cook!

CONTENTS

INTRODUCTION

SET THE PAGE ON FIRE

Set the Page on Fire: Secrets of Successful Writers will show you how to be a far more productive writer. When you set the page on fire, your writing takes off. Your readers catch fire, too, and keep reading as long as you burn.

This book will show you how to ignite a bonfire of writing and keep feeding it. You'll learn to recognize the writer's warm-up — and how to shift from your verbal brain to your writing brain. You'll learn tricks for getting hot fast, such as *puffensprachen*, in which you create a new word at the start of a writing session to ignite your massive written vocabulary.

Once you set the page on fire, the right words erupt effortlessly, like fireworks. You struggle to keep up with your thoughts instead of struggling to get started. You find yourself writing tweets, articles, emails, short stories, poems, screenplays, letters, and books! Your writing at work gets sharper, and even grocery lists start showing literary merit.

You'll want to find outlets for all this material, and this book will help you do that, too. You'll learn how to use the

Four-Part Pitch to shop your writing to websites, newspapers, magazines, journals, newsletters, and periodicals. The same pitch will put your work in front of top literary agents and book editors.

Once you learn to set the page on fire, you will no longer dread writing assignments — you'll look forward to them! You will no longer have trouble coming up with written material, even on a tight schedule. You'll love the way you write, and you'll want to write even more. You'll even look forward to the toughest writing assignment of all: pitching to editors and agents.

This book is based on interviews I conducted with two hundred and fifty successful authors and publishing professionals, and on my twenty-five years in the classroom teaching writing and publishing. It is also informed by my experiences as a freelance writer, the author of several textbooks, the editor of half a dozen newsletters, and the employer of dozens of successful writers.

Set the page on fire, and see how fast you learn to love what you write!

CHAPTER 1

TOP 10 SECRETS OF SUCCESSFUL WRITERS

Let's start right off with the Top 10 Secrets of Successful Writers, which are based on my interviews with published authors and book publishing professionals. (You can find a complete list of the authors interviewed at the back of the book, as well as video clips of most interviews at the companion website for *Set the Page on Fire*.) The Top 10 List below is shown in reverse order, followed by a summary and discussion of each secret. The secrets I am about to divulge will serve as handy reminders when you're in the heat of composition.

10. **Writing is discovery, not capture**
    It's something you kindle, not something you freeze.

9. **Schedule time at the keyboard**
    two hours/day = a book in a month
    one hour/day = a book in two months
    fifteen minutes/day = a book never

8. **Mechanics don't matter**
   Worry about writing quickly and getting across.

7. **A thousand words before dawn**
   The kids are still asleep, and you can write around your job.

6. **Write in Airplane Mode**
   The internet is designed to steal your time. Keep it turned off while you're writing.

5. **Don't talk about your writing**
   Talking damages desire. Your writing never comes out the way it sounds when you discuss it.

4. **Use the Four-Part Pitch**
   This is an effective short pitch for securing outlets for your writing.

3. **Know the person you're pitching to**
   Pitch to people, not companies. Show that you know who you're pitching to.

2. **Get it in writing**
   Get a commitment before you write.

1. **Tenacity**
   It can take eight years to break out, but it's worth it.

Let's examine each of these writing secrets in detail.

10. WRITING IS DISCOVERY, NOT CAPTURE

It's something you kindle, not something you freeze.

Summary: Many people think writing is a process of capturing thoughts. However, it is more a technique for growing thoughts than harvesting them. The best writing comes out of the process of discovery at the keyboard. It can rarely be thought out in advance and laid down whole.

Discussion: If you are serious about having your writing add up to something, you need to log hours at the computer (or pad of paper). It's hard to hold the entire text of an article or story in your mind until you get to a keyboard and let it all out. If you try to do so, what comes out is likely to sound all wrong. Why?

Your article dump sounds wrong because you created it in your mind, out of "brain language," which is largely self-talk. When you are forced to squeeze those ideas into the alphabet, they come out sounding like baby talk. The text is often dull and uninspiring, which makes it hard to get started.

Written pieces that are constructed in the mind and laid down whole are nearly identical to pieces dictated into a recorder and transcribed. Have you seen the machine transcriptions that online video services provide? The words used are small, incomplete, and confusing.

The speaking vocabulary for an English-language high school graduate consists of about ten thousand words. The same person's writing vocabulary is about forty thousand words. Her reading vocabulary is about fifty thousand words. These numbers are based on surveys of millions of people using vocabulary builder apps.

If you want to shape an article, a story, a report, a novel, or a poem, wouldn't you want a tool caddy of forty thousand words rather than an itty-bitty ten-thousand-word one? You set the page on fire when you ignite that big vocabulary at the keyboard. The writing goes so fast you can hardly keep up!

9. SCHEDULE TIME AT THE KEYBOARD

two hours/day = a book in a month
one hour/day = a book in two months
fifteen minutes/day = a book never

Summary: It takes only forty hours for an average typist to keyboard an average-length novel. So much for time as a barrier to getting that book written! If you put in two hours a day, five days a week, you will grow a book in one month. If it takes fifteen minutes to get "warmed up," as it does for many writers, then spending fifteen minutes a day writing is like clearing your throat but never singing.

Discussion: All the planning and thinking and researching you do disappears unless you spend time converting it into written language at the keyboard or with a pen. Since only the portion of your work that gets converted into language is writing, if you want to grow your writing output, schedule time to put your thoughts into writing.

Most writers have to defend that schedule against myriad intrusions in order to accomplish their goals. You need chunks of time from one to three hours long to make real progress with either articles or books. You need to pick a time of day you can stick to. You need a place where you won't be interrupted and where your writing won't disturb others. You need to find some method for evoking the muse and setting the page on fire so that your writing time is pleasant and productive.

The best way to call on the muse is to write a little every day. It doesn't matter what, really: emails, postcards, journal entries, to-do lists, blog posts, greeting cards, letters, memos, ideas, quotations, reviews — even text messages. Any conversion of thoughts into writing helps keep your muse close.

You set the page on fire by making the transition from your friendly but tiny verbal vocabulary to your massive, elegant written vocabulary. This book is full of tricks for getting into your writing vocabulary quickly, eliminating the writer's warm-up, and making your writing time significantly more productive.

8. MECHANICS DON'T MATTER
Worry about writing quickly and getting across.

Summary: Spend time perfecting your pitches, if you want, but not your writing. Writing reads better when it's done quickly, even if it contains errors. Writing that has been labored over is often so compact it's impenetrable. It's easy to fix writing that has bad mechanics, but it's very difficult to infuse ordinary writing with a voice that grabs the reader and a pace that doesn't let go.

Discussion: What draws people into reading a piece is wondering what's coming next. This sense of a reader's journey is baked right into the language itself: we read a few letters to recognize a word and a few words to make out a sentence. Just the process of understanding what is written is a path. Writers can harness the anticipation that is hardwired into the reading process to build suspense and compel attention.

You can generate this can't-wait-to-see-what-happens-next process when you, too, aren't sure of what's coming next and are working as fast as possible to type it out. When you are flying at the keyboard in this fashion, the writing is pleasant, even addictive, and the output can be tremendous. But the grammar sometimes suffers.

If you stop to fix problems in tense, sentence structure, spelling, and punctuation, it will slow your writing to a crawl. More of your sentences will come out perfectly — and be perfectly boring. If you lose the voice, the pace, the sense of discovery, you lose the reader. The writing becomes slow, unpleasant, laborious, predictable, and dull.

Write quickly. Use tricks to get yourself writing quickly. Don't worry about mechanics until you are done writing and in editing mode. When you write quickly and clean it up later, your writing will be stronger and more exciting, with a clearer voice and a better sense of direction.

7. A THOUSAND WORDS BEFORE DAWN

The kids are still asleep, and you can write around your job.

Summary: A surprising number of writers get their clicks in before sunrise. Since very few writers hit it big with their first book, they have regular jobs and must fit writing time into their working lives. Many successful authors use the hours before work to write, and they retain that schedule even after they become well known. Famous writers very often use the morning to compose, the afternoon for business, and the evening for inspiration.

Discussion: It can be just as hard to find the quiet to write as it is to find the time. When you write quickly, it feels as though you are listening to your own thought stream and turning it into text. If writing feels like listening, it makes sense that writers prefer quiet when they compose.

You can build mental walls to noise, as we all do when writing in a café or on a plane or train. You can build physical walls, too, by putting on headphones or closing a door. But there's nothing like real quiet to keep you writing for hours without noticing the passing of time.

Some writers get their quiet by going on retreats. Once you've seen how to set the page on fire, you can get a book written in as little as a week. An average typist can type an average-length novel in just forty hours at the keyboard. "That's not writing, that's typing," Truman Capote once quipped. But writing is, in fact, that portion of your thought that gets converted into alphabet. You can speed up that process when it's quiet.

Writing is easy compared with the administrative chores of being a professional author. When you find more outlets for your writing, you'll have more time for writing. Most successful authors give writing their first shot at the start of the day and spend the afternoon on business, once their creative fire has cooled.

6. WRITE IN AIRPLANE MODE
The internet is designed to steal your time. Keep it turned off while you're writing.

Summary: You don't need the internet to write an article or a book. It's very helpful for researching or editing, and that's when you should go online. Successful writers write fast, without interruption. They do research and editing in a separate pass. Believe it or not, it can be considerably faster to handwrite, use a typewriter, or speak an article than it is to keyboard the first draft on a computer that's online.

Discussion: Taking time to check facts as you write will destroy productivity. It's much better to leave markers for yourself about things you're not sure of than to stop each time to check them. Flow is everything to both writers and readers. You can feel it when you are in the zone, when writing is enjoyable and the words are coming faster than you can type them. There will be plenty of time to repair your grammar and check facts later, but there will never be another opportunity to give your writing the vital energy it needs to hold a reader's attention.

One way to write in Airplane Mode is to write your first drafts by hand. You can write almost anywhere; there is no temptation to fact-check or spell-check or grammar-check, so you can write very quickly — typically, twenty words a minute. You can edit the draft as you keyboard it and check facts at that time. Another way to stay offline is to use a typewriter for the first draft — typically, forty words a minute — then edit the draft and fact-check as you type the text into a computer. You can also keyboard the draft right into a computer but turn off the internet while you're writing or until you've hit your target word count.

You can even speak your writing into a dictation app on your phone or computer. I have several blind students who do just that. Until you get used to it, the written version can come out sounding like baby talk. The dictation has to be "translated" from spoken English into written English. The key to successful dictation is concentration — which is enhanced in Airplane Mode.

5. DON'T TALK ABOUT YOUR WRITING

Talking damages desire. Your writing never comes out the way it sounds when you discuss it.

Summary: Talking and writing are so profoundly different that talking about your writing will often ruin it. What appears on your computer monitor, or on the pad of paper, doesn't sound anything like what comes out of your mouth. Writing workshops are useful for motivating you to write, but they can be deadly if you start collecting too many spoken comments about your stories or articles. Look for cryptic, supportive mentors who comment only briefly, usually in writing, and often with notes of encouragement.

Discussion: Don't discuss your work verbally, even with experts — especially with experts — while your work is in progress. You can collect written comments, the best of which are brief enough and specific enough to be useful. You can share a piece of writing once it's almost finished, but don't smooth off the edges too much, or the writing will lose its personality.

The best part of your writing is going to be what you find, not what you think you'll find. It's going to sound a lot better when it's written, too, because you have such a well-endowed written vocabulary. Criticism is more meaningful when it's written, for the same reason. Transcribe the lecture of any successful writer, and she will sound as if she's talking nonsense — unless she's reading from a written script.

Writing a book is often compared to parenting. You treat your manuscript as something that needs privacy, to be sheltered from bright lights and loud noises, nourished with healthy food, kept away from chills, and read to by the fire at night. Only when this thing you are writing has its own personality should you expose it to review by another. At that point, you just want to hear how lovable it is.

When you restrain yourself from talking about your writing, you increase your desire to get to the page or the keyboard and get the ideas out. You will begin to see your writing time as akin to unwrapping a present: What could be in there? When you set the page on fire, every day is like Christmas Eve, it's that good.

4. USE THE FOUR-PART PITCH

This is an effective short pitch for securing outlets for your writing.

Summary: Pitching is one of the secrets of successful writers, and the Four-Part Pitch is a time-tested template for success. The four parts are stroke, pitch, credentials, and action alternatives. Using this pitch will significantly improve your acceptance rate for articles, essays, stories, and short pieces and lead you to editors and literary agents who can help you publish longer works. The Four-Part Pitch cuts the time spent trying to place your writing so you have more time to write. The Four-Part Pitch also generates steady referrals to new outlets.

Discussion: It doesn't necessarily take long to write a masterpiece, but it takes forever to get enough people to recognize your genius to sustain a print run of ten thousand copies. The best way to make time for writing is to cut the time spent on the administrative side of being a professional writer by using the extremely effective Four-Part Pitch.

This pitch has been tested literally millions of times. In the early days of the internet, there were only a few firms providing email news release services. Paul Krupin ran Internet Media Fax, I ran Internet Publicity Services, and we competed with PRWeb, PR Newswire, and Internet Wire. Paul and I often compared notes on the most effective pitches. Paul prefers using a story of overcoming adversity against incredible odds in pitches. I favor unabashed flattery in the opening line. I have used the pitch more than two thousand times, with average distribution of seven hundred contacts per pitch. That's 1.4 million email impressions.

The main things that kill email pitches are not focusing on the receiver, including too much information about you, including too much information about your project, including writing samples, and including links to anything. You want the receiver to ask for it. Once she asks you for something — anything — the relationship dynamics shift. Instead of you doing all the asking, the person receiving your pitch is asking for something from you. Keep her asking!

3. KNOW THE PERSON YOU'RE PITCHING TO

Pitch to people, not companies. Show that you know who you're pitching to.

Summary: Not knowing the person you're sending a pitch to is the number one biggest mistake beginning writers make. There are only one or two people who stand between you and professional publication: an editor and possibly a literary agent. What are their names? Have they been interviewed? Is there anything in their biographies you connect with? They are more likely to read your pitch if it begins with praise for their previous work.

Discussion: The most effective pitch begins with a statement of recognition that indicates to the reader that you have done your homework and that you know who you're pitching to. It can be as simple as using the person's name; many pitches don't. If you can genuinely connect with the reader in some way, that is the best way to get him to read the rest of your pitch.

Later on you'll learn some clever tricks for finding the names of people you should be sending pitches to. Once you locate the right people for your pitch, do your research. Learn as much as you can about them, and pour all that into the opening line. You should not mention your own project until you have paid homage to one of theirs.

After the pitch, leave room for a graceful exit. People change jobs. Should you contact someone else at the firm?

People change interests. Is there someone else who they think might want to see this pitch? Every pitch, if worded well, can be a source of referrals. The referral then becomes the opening line for the next pitch: "I was referred to you by Big Shot at Major Publishing House."

2. GET IT IN WRITING

Get a commitment before you write.

Summary: Professional writers usually pitch first, get commitments up front, and develop the ideas that get support, in that order. For articles, it can be as simple as suggesting a headline and getting a text back that says, "Go for it!" It's not necessarily a formal contract, and if the editors don't like the finished piece they usually won't pay for it. With books, the commitment can be a lengthy publishing agreement that involves a literary agent and an attorney. Book publishers often buy projects from established writers based on a pitch and a proposal. The writer can then tailor the book to the publisher's list.

Discussion: People who make a living as freelance writers often have a dozen projects in development at the same time. They are constantly pitching, writing, and submitting finished work. It's nice to have gigs in which you submit story ideas that get approved with little friction. It's also good to write in a variety of styles for a wide range of outlets because the diversity often leads to crossover discoveries, which are the kinds of insights people love to read about.

I've hired dozens of writers on specialized topics, and I like the ones who act like professionals. Because I am an intermediary for the client, it's more important to mc to have a project go smoothly than it is to get brilliant writing. I like writers who write fast, without worrying about the mechanics, and who do real research. I work with talented editors who can turn any scrap of quasi-English into a useful article, so good mechanics don't impress me.

Try to pitch three ideas at a time. If one gets a verbal or written commitment, develop it. When you turn it in, have three more ideas ready to go. It's possible to work entirely by commission, never going past twenty words without a payday or the promise of publication. Once you're famous, you can write the way you want whenever you want, and your reputation will ensure publication.

1. TENACITY

It can take eight years to break out, but it's worth it.

Summary: It takes, on average, eight years for a first-time author to get a book commercially published. You can self-publish instantly, of course, in which case it will likely take eight years to sell enough books to interest a commercial publisher. If you're writing short pieces, it will most likely take eight years to get enough name recognition to get an anthology published or to land a deal for a new book. The book you're holding now took twenty-five years to get published. I do not regret the time it took. In fact, almost every one of the two hundred and fifty published authors interviewed for this book do not regret the time, effort, or money invested to get published. A majority have written a second book, which they often get published in months, not years. It's a good sign that so many authors feel that the writing process has been time well spent.

Discussion: The most discouraging aspect of writing is the time it takes to get commercially published. Self-publication is instantaneous, but it comes with its own headaches of platforms, packaging, and distribution problems. Self-published books are shunned by reviewers and retailers until they prove themselves. Many self-published writers, once their projects are completed, feel like they were scammed or misled by unscrupulous vendors in the self-publishing space.

And yet, we persist. With all the costs and the headaches of getting established as a writer and/or self-publishing, almost all the people who have been through this process do not regret it. They consider being a published author one of the most important achievements of their lives. So even if it takes forever, and even if it costs way more than you expected, you are likely to have a smile on your face at the end of the ordeal.

All the tips you'll be picking up should dramatically cut the time it takes you to get commitments for writing projects and see them flower into publication. Most writers who get published want to be published even more. Authors who get published want to write a second book. Authors who self-publish want to leverage their learning curve, certain they will do better next time. It's a great sign that most of those who become published authors are eager to write their next book.

CHAPTER 2

YOU CAN DO THIS!

Brenda Ueland, author of *If You Want to Write*, a tremendously inspirational book on the writing craft, demonstrates why tenacity is the number one secret of successful writers. First published in 1938, the book disappeared until it was rediscovered and republished in the 1980s, when it became one of the bestselling books about the writing craft.

I was working as a book editor when I built a writing class for adults from Ueland's book and taught it at the local library. When I added a series on getting published, the classes were standing room only. So I landed a literary agent (using the Four-Part Pitch), and he circulated a book proposal for a sequel to Ueland's bestseller, based on my classes. Twenty-five years later, this original idea, grown through decades of teaching and hundreds of author interviews, became *Set the Page on Fire*.

"Everybody is talented, original and has something important to say" is Ueland's core message. I have worked with a huge variety of writers, including dozens of writers in prison, dozens of writers living overseas, hundreds of self-published authors, and hundreds of bestselling authors. I believe I have proof of Ueland's trinity that will help you realize that you have all the talent you need to write something that is both original and important.

Everybody Is Talented

What does it mean to have a talent for writing? How's this for a definition: to have a talent for writing is to have *a natural ability to write in a way that pleases others*. Let's break that definition down a little.

What does it mean to have *natural ability*? Does it mean "God-given"? None of us were born with the ability to write. Writing involves assembling the alphabet into words, words into sentences; it's a learned process. You can sing and be recognized as a talented singer without any voice training. You can paint and be recognized as a world-class painter without ever receiving any painting instruction. However, you cannot be a writer without having received instruction in how to string together the letters of the alphabet.

> You have all the talent you need to write something that is both original and important.

Another way to look at *natural ability* is to see it as affinity: writing is something you enjoy doing. You take to it readily and easily. I think anyone would enjoy writing if she knew what writing really was. But many people sit down to compose and hear all sorts of nagging voices in their heads: teachers scolding them about person or tense; papers returned with a D on them because the teacher didn't like it (or didn't like *you*); siblings telling you your story stinks or is not as good as Jane's — "she's the real talent in the family"; parents saying "that's nice" as they set aside the poem you brought home, later using it as a drink coaster; bosses who mark up your best efforts with a red pen and encourage you to be less personal, or do more research, or break out *Strunk & White*.

Of course you have the Strunks and Whites of the world in the back of your mind, or even right in front of you: the dictionary (be careful to spell everything correctly), the thesaurus (find better words), *The Chicago Manual of Style* (should that semicolon go inside or outside the quotation marks?). Given all these rules, these experts, these naysayers in our heads, it's a wonder anyone enjoys writing.

People with a natural talent for writing are not experts in punctuation, grammar, and spelling. They're experts in *communicating* by using the alphabet. People who enjoy writing are those who can push those experts and critics out of their heads and fly along merrily at the keyboard, anxious to see what comes next. Writing is a way to see inside ourselves, inside other people, inside the world around us. Many people are fascinated to make these discoveries and enjoy the process of bringing them out through writing.

As soon as we learn the alchemy of the alphabet, the wonder of words, we join the club of writers. All you need to be a talented writer is to accurately describe what you are thinking and feeling.

I volunteer as a technology coach at a senior living center near my home. One of the people I work with has Parkinson's disease and is in danger of becoming "locked in," unable to effectively communicate his needs. He's very intelligent and uses a computer every day, but his eyesight is deteriorating, so we practice using screen magnifiers. He has lost the dexterity in his fingers and is down to one-handed, one-finger typing. The disease has attacked his ability to speak clearly. People cannot understand him and find it difficult to converse with him. He still has good mobility in his feet, however, so I outfitted his wheelchair with a foot mouse for his computer. If he wanted to, he could write his autobiography with his feet.

As a child Helen Keller developed her own interior language, but she did not know how to write. She knew what she wanted to eat and where she wanted to be, but she lacked any effective way of sharing that knowledge, until Anne Sullivan showed her how to attach her ideas to symbols, which she traced in Keller's hand. Within twenty-four hours, young Helen Keller had attached the words in her mind to symbols. That's how she learned to write: by making shapes in her own hand or in the hand of another person.

Keller went on to learn to read and write in Braille, an alphabet based on patterns of raised dots that can be read by running the fingertips across the dots. She also learned how to type on a standard QWERTY-style keyboard, as do most blind students in America today. She wrote hundreds of articles and numerous books during her lifetime. We all have obstacles we must overcome to get our writing done, but no barrier should prevent you from expressing in writing what is inside you.

I also volunteer as a tech coach at the Virginia School for

the Deaf and the Blind in Staunton, Virginia, where many years ago I worked with a student who was partially blind and cognitively impaired in a most perplexing way. He could not type the word *cat*, but he could set up a virtual private network in the cloud and show you how to encrypt your email. He asked for my help promoting his YouTube videos, and I pointed out that his videos lacked any keywords or descriptive text that would allow people to find them using a search engine.

The next week, I came to the assistive technology lab and saw that my student had added text descriptions and keywords to his videos on YouTube. The instructor looked over our shoulders and gasped, "How did you do that? Did someone write those for you?"

"No," he said, worried he'd done something wrong.

"Well, how did you get that description in there? You didn't type it, did you?" the teacher asked.

"No," he said. "I did it with Siri," meaning the voice recognition app that's built into most Apple devices.

Here is the process my student used. He would speak his description into a text message or email. He would then have his computer read it back to him using a screen reader, and when the description sounded right, he would copy it and paste it into YouTube. The writing was phonetically correct and easy to understand. He had never displayed an ability to write before this. His teacher was stunned at his clever solution. This is a method we now teach to many blind students: use a dictation program to speak your writing, then use a screen reader to hear it read back until it is right. Many blind people are able to generate peer-level papers using this method.

If you can put words on paper or screen and convey meaning with those words — and everyone who has language can do this — you've got talent. Are there some folks who are just better alphabet stringers and word slingers than others? Yes, but not because they are more talented. It's because they're more practiced, more authentic, more careful. To suggest that some writing is "good" and other writing is "bad" is to imply a scale where none exists except personal taste. The issue is not good versus bad but whether the writing communicates or not — whether it gets across.

Everybody Is Original

Fortunately, you cannot help but be original; it is one of the tragedies of the human condition. Each of us is fundamentally alone in what we experience and how it affects us. I call it a tragedy because no matter how close we get to someone, we still can't see things exactly the same way he does. There is some confusion. Things get lost in translation. People get misunderstood.

No two people see the same thing the same way. Ask any police officer what it's like interviewing witnesses to an automobile accident. Sometimes their stories are so different it's hard to believe they're describing the same event. The first assignment in the writing class I teach is to describe an object placed on the table at the front of the room. Here are what two students wrote the night I used a red rose in a glass vase:

WRITER ONE

a deep rose full blown
past its prime? It has a
lot to teach…
It has seen glorious secret days.
It can reminisce even as its
petals fall.…

WRITER TWO

I think if I were living in the seventeenth century, I
would appreciate the flower before me much more
than I do now. It looks boring. Boring and trite.
Right down to the slender vase it sits in. I feel like I've
seen it a million times before, either plastic or live.

These two writers are describing the same object in the
same place at the same time. Their descriptions of the rose
reflect their perceptions of the world. No two people will ever
describe the rose the same way. For another class, I used my
favorite hat for this exercise. One writer called it "a scruffy
crown for a down and out king," and another wrote, "Face-
less men walking, staring, drawn gray like the felt. You can
see the eyes of them, they burn."

No matter how hard we try, we cannot help but be original. All we can ever know about the things outside ourselves
comes through our senses. We can describe the color, shape,
texture, weight, taste, and smell of objects, but our impressions of these objects will be different from anyone else's. As
writers, as long as we are accurately expressing our thoughts

and feelings, they will be unique. We all have something of value to contribute.

What Does Your Moon Look Like?

Think about it. Almost all of us have the ability to see the moon most nights of the year. And this has been true throughout recorded history. What does the moon look like to you?

There have been thousands of references to the moon in literature and millions of renditions of the moon in art — possibly *billions* when you consider the number of children who have drawn the moon at some time during childhood. Every one of those drawings is different — unique. And any description of the moon longer than, say, fifty words is likely to be unique. When you try to tell me something about how the moon looks to you, and you keep at it for a while, you cannot help but tell me something about you, about how you see the world, possibly about how you see *yourself* in the world. That is the power of language — the power of expression.

If you give me only two words about the moon, it's a little tricky to divine anything about your personality. Maybe it means you're brief? We know a quarter moon and a crescent moon, a full moon and a new moon, a half moon, a harvest moon, a blue moon. Most of your readers will have well-established associations with those terms. At the simple two-word level, readers are not seeing *your* moon so much as one of their own, pressed into service in order to move along in the text. You have to be original to communicate much with a two-word moon. Maybe "fish moon," indicating that phase between the third quarter and the new moon when the moon is shaped like a silver fish leaping from a black sea?

When you stretch out in your writing and give us the details of what you are seeing or hearing or feeling, you can't help but be original. Your writing acquires personality, and that glimpse into your personality is the payoff for readers. We begin to see the way your mind works, and it helps us to get through difficult passages in your writing and extract a common line — the voice of you, the author.

Yes, readers can get a mistaken impression of you. They can be wrong when they try to intuit things about your personality from a simple description of the moon. But whose fault is that, the writer's or the reader's? Readers cannot help but build an inadequate impression of the author — *no one can know you through your writing alone* — because that writing is itself an abstraction, a distillation of the thought, and you are limited to expressing that thought process through a chintzy alphabet and some formatting tricks.

Readers may buy a book because of the promise, but they read a book because they are drawn in. They stick with it because they are anxious to find out what happens next. I don't think there is any facet of writing that draws in readers faster and holds them more securely than an honest search for the truth.

You don't have to be a blabbermouth to get your personality across while searching for the truth. You don't have to write fifty-word descriptions of every insect that lands on your window. Your writing doesn't have to be the literary equivalent of an MRI scan, exploring every millimeter of a very long trip. Some readers don't go in for microscopic detail and want the author to keep going and to quit stopping to smell all the stupid flowers already.

Individuality does require clarity. An image clearly seen

can often be expressed economically. *Fish moon* is only two words. Since I have already described it to you, I can say "fish moon" now and you know what I mean. In fact, I defy you to look at the moon some night when it is between the third quarter and the new moon, and not think of *fish moon* and somewhere in the back of your skull remember faintly the paragraph you are reading right now. It is just that easy to put a spell on readers.

Sometimes the most microscopically detailed writing is the most economical, too. When I'm editing books, I often wish the author would just give us an example and spare us the lecture. One well-wrought illustration of a bumblebee having sex with a buttercup can tell us more about the origins of the species than the collected works of Charles Darwin. The great universal truths are often revealed in their imperfect application to a particular situation. Show me that situation, and I will find the thread and run it through the rest of your economical prose.

WRITING EXERCISE
YOUR MOON

What does *your* moon look like? You don't need a notebook; there's enough room in the margins for you to write a fifty-word description, more or less. Write it on the back of an envelope or some other handy scrap of paper. You don't need to think about it too much — just give me fifty words on the moon. Right now.

When you are finished rendering your moon, send it to me if you like, and I will post it on the web — anonymously, if you want. Send it by email or snail mail, and come see what other people's moons look like. Given a fifty-word description, and no cheating, I could have thousands of moons on my site without a single duplication. Isn't that amazing! I'll keep posting these as long as I'm receiving enough of them to keep it interesting. So why don't you write about your moon right now, and send it to me tomorrow?

Everybody Is Valuable

Of the three legs of Brenda Ueland's philosophy, it is this last item that is probably most difficult to prove: "Everybody has something important to say." Yes, you say, I have the ability to feel and the ability to express those feelings in writing. Yes, you say, I suppose my writing is original — maybe too original — because it is not identical to anyone else's. But is what I write really important? Is anybody's writing really important? Would it make much of a difference to the world if I did not write?

Yes, yes, and yes!

Imagine what your life would be like now if you had never read a single book. Now take away all the magazines and newspapers, and keep going until you get to the very first sentence, and take that away, too. Now take away the internet, the television, the radio, the sound of music, the sound of a human voice. What kind of person would you be then? I'll tell you what I see: a brute squatting naked under a tree, crying, feeling *these things*, feeling this desire to express them and have them heard; and from his tortured face comes a painful, prolonged moan. And that becomes the first word upon which this thing we call language is built.

Writing, making music, making art — these are all forms of expression. We see something or hear something or feel something, and we try to capture it or record it or transmit it, for our own benefit and perhaps for the benefit of others. But all expression is symbolic; that is, it is an interpretation of what we are feeling, hearing, or seeing and not the thing itself. It is an extraction, an opinion, a point of view — more unique, even, than our DNA.

When you take the trouble to share your view with me, it broadens my world. I am richer for it. I may hate it, and that is good; the wind makes no sound without something to rub against. Sometimes we don't know what to believe until we find something we disagree with, and then at least we know it's not that. I may love your view, and that's better. Your words may inform me, inspire me. I might be indifferent, but that would more likely be my failing as a listener, not yours as a writer. I might think I've heard your song before — there is nothing new in it. If that's true, it's because you haven't taken enough care to accurately express what you are feeling, seeing, or hearing. When you do, there is always something new in it, something I can learn from, because you cannot help but be original. No one sees the world exactly as you do. When you share your vision as honestly as possible, and I read it as openly as possible, I cannot help but be changed.

Do you realize what this means? If you had a million people staring at the same tree, each of us would have a slightly different view of what we're seeing. It's the same tree, but a million different visions — if we are all honest and detailed in expressing what we see — and none of these visions is "wrong." One tree becomes one million trees, and every one of them is both different and accurate! It's a miracle, like multiplying loaves and fishes. Yet that's the world we live in.

Now I ask you to indulge me just a bit further, and look about you and tell me what you see. Are you sitting in a chair, lying in bed, riding the subway? Are you in a house, a car, a library? Do you realize that everything in the space around you — the lamp, the table, your reading glasses, your clothing — all of it *has always been there*. That's right! Matter cannot be created or destroyed, it can only change shape. All the material in the universe has always been here. The only thing missing has been the knowledge to make it change shape.

Where will that knowledge come from? That's right — from you. From you having the courage to say what you see, and the patience to try to get it right. Do you think your writing is not important? How has your life been shaped by the things you have read? How has your unique perspective, written or not, changed the lives of the people around you? What a loss it would be not to have your vision added to the mix. And what a loss to *you* if you did not attempt to express yourself in writing.

I once interviewed the world's most famous book publishing management consultant, John Huenefeld, author of *The Huenefeld Guide to Book Publishing*, on assignment for a periodical. He pointed out what a minuscule impact publishing has on the gross national product:

Across the interstate from my office in Bedford, Massachusetts, is the world headquarters of the Raytheon Corporation....Sometimes I look out the window toward the freeway and realize that the gross revenue of this one company exceeds the entire annual revenues of all the US book publishers combined. But look at the impact these publishers have had! They've changed the way we think, the way we dress, the way we act. They've led the peace movement, civil rights, equal rights for women, religious freedom, the environmental movement. They've toppled world leaders, stopped wars, and shared the knowledge that fueled the new economy. They have changed the world. That's something.

If you read this book without doing the exercises and making words on paper, I will be heartbroken. How do you know that your careful description might not lead to a cure for AIDS, or unleash the next Beethoven, or bring someone back from the brink of suicide, or that the person you saved might not parent the next Mohandas Gandhi? We can never know the repercussions our writing will have in the world, because every reader gets something unique and personal out of your prose (or poetry). What you *can* know is how writing affects you. If you fail to write, you are denying yourself one of the sublime pleasures of living: to feel something, to fix it in your heart by trying to express it, to carry it with you all the days of your life.

So, please, make your life richer by writing about it, and

make the reader's life richer by sharing your writing. It's just that simple.

Everybody Is Perishable

Though this last section is not part of Brenda Ueland's writing trinity, it must be said. We are all leaving the planet sometime soon. You need to say what you're going to say in writing before the opportunity passes by. That's why I'm so anxious that you send me some of your writing. I'm not kidding. Actually, you don't have to send it to me, but you do have to write!

My father passed away in 2003. He believed I had talent as a writer and always encouraged me. "You should be a writer," he would say, and I would explain to him that I write several hours a day, every day, I get bylined articles published every month, and clients pay handsomely for my news releases. In the decades since I left Michigan, I had built a successful business doing online publicity for book publishers, I had written two textbooks on internet publicity for John Wiley & Sons, I was teaching internet public relations at Tulane University, and I was doing PR for Dr. Seuss! "You know what I mean," he would say. "You should write books."

So I decided to take a summer off, go back to Port Townsend, Washington, and write down all the stories I had gathered from editing the work of prison inmates for a decade and teaching writing for a decade. I returned to New Orleans three months later with a nearly finished manuscript and a new business plan. I would leave New Orleans every summer, travel the country interviewing authors, then take the video back to New Orleans to be edited and uploaded to the internet.

I completed the manuscript for the writing book by the end of the year and sent it to my literary agent. As the end of the school year approached, I purchased a used Ford Econo-line van and tricked it out with a mobile production studio. The van was the home of my new business: AuthorViews videos of authors introducing their books. In June 2005 we took off in search of authors to film, traveling to Houston, Austin, Santa Fe, Salt Lake City, Seattle, San Francisco, Los Angeles, and San Antonio. We returned to New Orleans with forty-eight author interviews ready to go into editing.

Hurricane Katrina arrived a few days later.

I loaded the manuscript, rough draft, and raw materials for the writing book into two plastic waterproof file boxes and put them into the van. I took all the AuthorViews video-tapes and signed releases and put them in the van as well. I handed my condo keys to two of my neighbors and told them to help themselves. I picked up my ex-wife and her friend, who was visiting from Port Townsend, and we drove out of New Orleans Sunday night at the end of a long line of traffic just before they closed the freeways.

On Monday, August 29, my six employees lost all their possessions and their homes. I watched the drama unfold from my daughter's house in Nashville, Tennessee. On about day three, the kerosene storage facility next to my office in New Orleans caught fire. All through the night, kerosene cyl-inders shot like rockets into a black sky without streetlights. There was no water pressure with which to put the fire out. A fire boat on the Mississippi River eventually soaked the remains of the warehouse with river water. Unfortunately, they accidentally soaked part of my office, too.

I returned to New Orleans a week later with plywood, tarps, water, gloves, coveralls, cell phone chargers, disposable cell phones, Neosporin, and for the checkpoints, bourbon and cigarettes. New Orleans was under mandatory evacuation, but the white Econoline got me through the checkpoints because I looked like FEMA. Nothing was missing from my office. I loaded up as much gear as I could and gave the booze and the cigarettes to the National Guard, but they still would not let me leave because of the curfew. I had to sleep on the levee while the Guard took turns chasing off stray dogs. In the morning I left for my brother's place in Richmond, Virginia.

Two months later, when New Orleans lifted the mandatory evacuation, I loaded up the van and went back down the Appalachian Highway to join my fellow writers and publishers at the New Orleans Bookfair, the first cultural event in the city since Katrina. We set up the cameras and filmed interviews nonstop. We cut them down and sent a collection out to media outlets as *The Katrina Tapes*. You can see them all at the website for this book.

After Katrina, I became obsessed with interviewing authors. We filmed at the Tennessee Williams Festival in New Orleans, the Virginia Festival of the Book (VABook) in Charlottesville, and the BookExpo America in New York. We filmed a dozen interviews at Gibbs Smith Publisher in Salt Lake City and another dozen at Berrett-Koehler Publishers in San Francisco. Thanks to Maureen Walsh at Life Works Books, we filmed more than a dozen authors in Santa

Fe, New Mexico. We toured in the summer of 2006. We toured in the summer of 2007.

At the end of the 2007 tour, we all got together in the same room at the same time for the first time in two years! And guess what? No one wanted to work out of the office anymore. We liked life on the road, and we had gotten good at it. So I closed the office and moved the plastic boxes with this manuscript and the videotapes into safekeeping.

One thing all the AuthorViews authors had in common — regardless of how they had been published and their age, ethnicity, gender, and so on — was that they uniformly agreed they want to write another book! That's how strong the oxytocin of publishing is! That should convince you that your instinct to write is true, that you will not regret the writing project you have in mind, and that you should get started on it right away.

When you are a published author — and you will be on the way to being published by the time you finish this book, if you want to be — I hope I have the opportunity to interview you. Because you are talented, you are original, you are valuable — and you are perishable. If you do not get it said, and soon, you might not get another chance. The world would be a smaller place without your contribution.

CHAPTER 3

LISTENING FOR GOOD WRITING

One of the biggest barriers to writing is the feeling that we are not qualified or competent to write. We cannot find the words to express what we want to say. We feel that our vocabulary is not up to the task we have set for ourselves. Or we start to string words together, and when we pause to take stock of what we have written, we are embarrassed. It doesn't speak. It doesn't add up. And so we stop.

Everyone who can read is qualified to write and capable of crafting something in print that is powerful and important. Here's the story of Robert the Dog. It has helped many men and women in my writing classes overcome the fear of writing and get down to business making marks on the page. They all remember Robert the Dog, and he reminds them not to fuss so much over their writing. The following paragraphs are from a letter to the editor in the *Port Townsend Leader*.

Who Killed My Dog Robert in His Bed?

May I take this opportune time to thank the local merchants and the Post Office for allowing me to post signs for my missing pet doggie, Robert? Also, to the Bayshore Animal Shelter Society advising me to keep a positive attitude assured, the tender help from PAWS, and a beautiful letter from KCTS about not giving up on finding Robert.

It was not satisfying deep in my heart, but the thought that "just maybe" Robert was stolen for a pet in a new home, and not suffering in some laboratory helped. A suggestion was made to put an ad in the local newspaper, which I did. The Reeds were wonderful to allow me to use their address for possible contacts.

Robert barked pathetically at the gorgeous stand of forest trees felled at a nearby clearing. He was in reality calling "Save that tree!" We both shivered as each tree hit the ground making a horrendous groan. Later the dozer clearing sent our little house into an earthquake-like tremor, and then again. Many earth vibrations followed making a window rattle. Thus, Robert barked. His bark was one of pity and to save our place. No one complained to us.

I'm sure Robert knew he was going to die. He wanted to tell me in the worst way, but I could not understand what he meant. I was probably not listening. That night of July 26, Robert barked furiously as though someone was coming onto the porch where he slept. And then he was quiet. He was not there the next morning.

Just last week, I was airing and laundering Robert's bed for the loving new pet Bayshore delivered to me, and we loved each other instantly. Then I found a one-inch hole, a burned hole in his pillow. I held it in my hands a long time in disbelief. It was definitely a bullet-hole. I pulled the box into the sunshine to see blood at the bottom.

ROBERT WAS SHOT IN HIS HOUSE. His bed was his safe-haven, and it was there he was cornered, without a chance of survival. I weep.

One day I picked up an orange-red shell on the other side of the porch, which left a strange feeling as it looked rather new.

Who? Who was standing there outside my door that Thursday night, holding a gun at my cornered little doggie? Who? Why? Where is his body?

My Robert who danced with my grandchildren, and delighted the folks in the nursing home on our visits. He was always happy, with his tail wagging. Birds stopped singing. I thought you caring people would want to know.

Good-bye Robert.

Every week, this newspaper publishes more than five thousand column inches of writing. This letter is the finest piece of writing I have found, after viewing more than a million column inches in this paper. Yet look how crude the construction is. The author doesn't use complete sentences.

She rambles. Her subjects and objects are all mixed up. In several places, it's difficult to know what she's trying to say. The structure is tortuous. It's difficult for this woman to use written language to convey meaning. And yet the piece speaks.

When she says, "Birds stopped singing," I believe her. When she makes the simple two-word sentence "I weep," I find myself weeping, too. Some say it's easy to make powerful prose out of tragic situations. What is more clearly illustrated here is that one can communicate effectively in writing while breaking all the rules — just by sticking to the truth. This woman is a talented writer. Her talent is her honesty.

All you have to do to be a successful writer is to tell the truth, as you see it, and it will be recognized as such and be moving to the reader. "The writer has a feeling and utters it from his true self. The reader reads it and is immediately infected," wrote Brenda Ueland, to which I'll add: *Write sincerely and honestly, and you will be understood.* Let me share another example of how bad writing can communicate well and get commercially published.

Bad Writing That Is Actually Good

This example comes from a book I edited while working at Loompanics Unlimited, a publisher of counterculture books. Many Loompanics authors were living behind bars. Quite a few did not want their real names associated with their books — only with the checks resulting from sales of those books. In the case of "Bruce Easley," author of *Biz-Op*, all my written communications went through a mail drop, and all my verbal communications went through a telephone answering service. I had no idea where this author lived. "Bruce" had good reasons for keeping his whereabouts secret.

The full title of his book is *Biz-Op: Business Opportunity Frauds and Scams*. Bruce made his living bilking people out of their savings. The law was after him, but it wasn't the law he was worried about. He was more concerned that his "investors" might hurt or even kill him if they caught him. At least that's what he told me — if you can believe anything a con man tells you. If you are successful at any criminal activity for very long, you come to the attention of organized crime, and then you have real trouble. But I'm getting ahead of the story. Here is a sample of Bruce's writing:

> When you have finished securiing your charity locations, you will need to collect the rest of your locateing money.
>
> If you are puting in charity honor boxes you just simpley turn the location list over to the mooch and collect what is do you. You do not tour mooch's with charity honor boxes, but make sure all your adress are correct.
>
> Charity C.T. vends are a differant story. You will have to tour your mooch, but try to avoid takeing him into the location. If you take the mooch in, the store owner might say, "This is only for 30 days. Right?" Your mooch, who is expecting his vending machine to stay in forever, will not want to hear that.
>
> In order to prevent this I tell the mooch that I have explained to the location that a representative of the charity will be in to place the vending

machine....By telling the mooch this it alivates the nessity of introdiceing him to the location owner, Instead of takeing the mooch inside you just Point his locations out as you are driveing by. Once you have finished the tour you turn the charity contracts over to the mooch and collect your money.

If the above four paragraphs survived my publisher's spellchecker and copyeditor, you would be laughing right about now — or shaking your head in amazement. I have my original, copyedited version of these four paragraphs. It has forty-three corrections or changes marked in red pen on it. You're worried you don't have enough command of the language to express yourself adequately in writing? If this guy can get commercially published, so can you.

The reason Bruce Easley got published is that his writing *does* communicate well. You can feel the love for the customer ("mooch"), can't you? You can tell how important the money is, can't you? Even out of context, you can tell there's a double con going on here, a fraud being perpetrated against both the "mooch" and the "location." But there's no fraud against the reader: this is the real deal. Bruce is telling his version of the truth the best way he knows. You can't make up stuff like this — in its raw state, as illustrated above, it is beyond the imagination of a novelist. Good writing "alivates the nessity" of mechanics; it transcends them, it surpasses the page and goes right for your nervous system. The only good writing comes from you telling your truth as quickly and economically as possible.

Bruce Easley didn't get published because of what he did for a living; he got published because of *how he wrote* about what he did for a living. When you tell the truth in a way that is natural to you, people will recognize the power of your writing and be grateful you shared your vision with them. How many publishers would have rejected Bruce's writing after a superficial examination revealed his nearly phonetic spelling and casual grammar? Lots of great writing is rejected, but a lot percolates through — it's hard to hold back powerful prose from reaching a reader. So stop worrying about whether you have the command of language needed to carry off your project. Just get out the paper and keep putting words on it, and you'll quickly see that I'm right about this.

> The only good writing comes from you telling your truth as quickly and economically as possible.

Bruce received an advance against royalties. His manuscript was cleaned up and published. It sold fairly well, mostly to police departments, better business bureaus, credit card companies, fraud units, and screenplay writers. He received royalty checks every six months while the book was in print. He appeared on a nationally televised daytime talk show as an expert on work-from-home scams. In forty-eight hours, he managed to bilk the talk show out of several thousand dollars in meal, bar, and limo charges.

Good Writing That Is Actually Bad

Good writing has little to do with proper grammar, accurate punctuation, competent sentence structure, or mechanics in general. In fact, polish and sophistication often work against writing and sabotage communication. Take a look at this example:

And just as there's a privileged co-occurrence between fixed subjects and variable characters, fixed verbs and variable actions, so we claim that there's a privileged co-occurrence in this geography of paragraphs and higher-level structures.

Huh? Yes, this sentence is taken out of context. But it's a complete sentence and, even in context, a complete disaster. You might expect to see rigorous phrasing like this in a book on physics. But even complex subjects can be dealt with fluently, even grippingly. Unschooled readers can appreciate Einstein's descriptions of the theory of relativity. Pieces on complex subjects are only hard to follow when the writer is not up to the task, unable to clearly communicate the subject at hand. Overblown language like this is often the result of a writer attempting to hide his or her ignorance behind a wall of words.

What is the source of the atrocious sentence copied out above? It comes from the journal *Writing on the Edge*, published by the Campus Writing Center at the University of California, Davis. The masthead indicates that the journal is a member of the "Conference of Editors of Learned Journals."

WRITING EXERCISE
OVERBLOWN PHRASING

Find a scrap of paper and something to write with. Copy down a beloved maxim or phrase, such as "par for the course" or "every dog has his day." Then see if you can puff it up to maximum volume without losing the thread of the idea.

This exercise will help improve your sensitivity to overblown phrasing in your own work. While I don't recommend making a study of bad writing when there is so much good writing to inspire us, it doesn't hurt to note terrible phrasing when you come across it accidentally, and to copy it into a journal of quotations, if you're in the habit of keeping such a record.

Keeping a Fake Book

When you *do* find writing of merit — writing that makes you stop and take notice — celebrate that and meditate on how the writer accomplished his or her little trick of getting you to pause in the mediocrity of everyday life to hear a well-tuned phrase.

I worked as a copywriter for many years and kept a file of good commercial writing to inspire me before I sat down to compose. My favorite example of junk mail poetry came from the Edge Company, a retailer of knives in Brattleboro, Vermont. What a challenge it must be to write about hundreds of almost identical-looking products yet make each one sound unique. A knife is basically a blade that is sharp on one side and dull on the other, and has a handle. Yet the copywriters at the Edge Company took to the task with good humor and inventiveness, going beyond making each item sound unique and using the power of language to make you lust to hold one. Here are a few excerpts from a piece of junk mail they sent me:

Bonded polymers of stress port black Nylex combine with scalpel edged unichromatic steel — achieving near weightlessness in the process. The result is a slender pocket rocket of seven-inch one-handed action.

Twin streaks of pure abalone shell are cut, polished, and fused to seven inches of heat brazened satin steel. A knife of fast and piercing beauty.

I'm not even into knives, but this writing is almost good enough to make me order one. I'll stick with the sharp copywriting, though, and leave the actual cutting devices for the knife enthusiasts out there.

I know the term *fake book* from the world of music. A musician's fake book contains sheet music, most often for a wide variety of popular songs or so-called standards. To hold as many songs as possible, fake books usually contain only *lead sheets* — the basic melody line and/or chord changes for the tune. Lead sheets are like the outline of a tune; it's the musician's job to add the embellishments.

I recommend that you keep a reader's Fake Book of Favorite Quotations. You may be doing this already in some fashion. When I read, I try to keep my ears open for phrasing that delights. I underline quotes, dog-ear pages, and copy things out into my fake book when I'm finished reading. Sometimes I'll copy out whole paragraphs or pages, trying to divine a writer's technique in creating statements so well made. If I write a book review for publication, I almost always include a long quote that illustrates the writer's talent. Here is a line from Brenda Ueland's *If You Want to Write*: "Get out truthfully what is in you, and it will be interesting."

And here's a nice passage from a book Ueland recommends, *The Letters of Vincent van Gogh*: "Believe me, in things of art the saying is true: Honesty is the best policy; rather more trouble or a serious study than a kind of *chic* to flatter the public. Sometimes in moments of worry I have longed for some of that *chic*, but thinking it over I say: No, oh, let me be true to myself, and in a rough manner express severe, rough, but true things."

Here is one more sound bite from my fake book on the issue of writing and truthfulness, by comedian and *Daily Show* host Trevor Noah: "The best comedy is informed by the truth." Many successful writers, especially screenwriters, think of their writing as a stand-up routine. It can help motivate you to think of your writing time as a performance on your own show.

Quotations often contain the distilled essence of an author's ideas or style. Just reading a quote from my fake book can sometimes bring an entire book back into view, just as glancing at a lead sheet can inspire a musician to remember a favorite rendition of a particular tune.

For centuries copying out favorite passages and poems in longhand has been a common way to enjoy books. In 2007 I interviewed author Jonathan Gross at VABook in Charlottesville. He's the scholar behind *Thomas Jefferson's Scrapbooks: Poems of Nation, Family, and Romantic Love Collected by America's Third President*. Jefferson's fake books were among his most prized possessions. He gave them to his granddaughters, and for a long time scholars thought the granddaughters had assembled them. Gross traced them back to Thomas Jefferson and showed how lines from these poems and ideas from these passages had made their way into Jefferson's writings.

Collecting a writer's best lines, either by copying them out in longhand or typing them in, can impart an understanding of an author's technique that will inform your own writing. The quotations you copy down will find their way into your own writing, along with ideas inspired by them. But please note: You cannot use these quotations in published works without first getting permission. Nowadays publishers run every item they publish through copy-protection software to find uncredited quotations, also known as plagiarism. So be diligent about keeping a fake book and careful about using the quotations properly.

Listening Exercises

Good writers write well, and great writers listen well. Writing is first an act of listening. Experience enters your consciousness and is converted into words that are spoken first, silently, to yourself, as thoughts. Writing begins by listening well to yourself and converting what you hear into alphabet — letters and words that tumble onto the page, linking up into phrases and sentences that capture the spirit of our thoughts in our crude but commonly shared calligraphy. Any listening practice improves the writer, whether it's listening intently to conversation or music or nature. Stories are being told all the time. It's easy to fail to listen intently to any of it, letting it wash over you without thought or examination — a sea of sounds emanating from every corner of existence.

I began consciously focusing my listening through *listening exercises* about fifteen years ago. They always begin with the same instruction: *Write down everything you can hear right now.* A listening exercise from a café might include snippets of conversation, the clattering of dishes, the linear percussion of a credit card machine printing out a receipt. At the beach you might attempt to describe the sound of a wave falling, which is actually not one sound but a sequence, like all sounds. Here is a listening exercise I made on a sweltering summer day in New Orleans. Notice how it starts descriptively but quickly takes a more literary turn:

Write down everything you can hear right now.
It begins with the soft tolling of the church bells
knocking off the hour from St. Mark's on Rampart
Street.

Next there is the hum of air conditioners.
Behind that, the whine of central air units in the
courtyard–
four of them, running nonstop, 24/7.

The breeze has its own form of chatter today,
leaves whispering among themselves.
You are grateful for any wind they send your way.

From the hallway downstairs
the painters blast their music as they work.
They speak a native tongue,

a patois of French-inflected English
laced with obscenities and peculiarities.

Every day they make a lot of noise:
hammering and gasping air compressors,
laughing and fighting and dropping things.

Listening exercises done in busy urban environments are filled with efforts to describe the difference between the sounds of motors: the baritone of the diesel truck as opposed to the whine of a scooter.

WRITING EXERCISE
LISTENING

Write down everything you can hear right now, in detail.

As writers, we are trying to put experience and thoughts into words. It's good practice to hunt for words that capture an experience or thought *exactly* — at least for you, and hopefully for your readers. In this attempt to be specific, we often discover what we have to contribute as a writer: our unique vision.

If you're very specific, you will write about the sound of a dog barking in a way no one else ever has. You hear it differently. The air around you may carry the sound quickly to your ears or muffle it with moisture. Even the shape of your ear is unique, its chambers reflecting the vibrations in a pattern no other human being shares. Of course your dog is different from any other, and so is the sound of its bark. Your way of associating that sound — that it's like the pop of a plunger leaving the throat of the kitchen sink or the laugh of a hyena drunk with blood — is unique and tells us something about you while advancing the story for the reader.

Listening exercises are a versatile tool for drilling down with language to arrive at a more exact expression of experience. You can do listening exercises on people, places, or things — characters in your stories, favorite cities, love.

30-Up Cliché Buster

One time I wanted to write a listening exercise at the beach and I had no paper. I did have a sheet of 30-up mailing labels, so I composed on that. It led to a series of 30-up listening exercises: fill the page, and you're done.

One of the best uses for a 30-up listening exercise is maneuvering around clichés. Cliché is the great enemy of writers. It consists of substituting someone else's vision for your own. It is probably best not to stop your writing flow to fix clichés when they happen, but you will want to find these in editing and fix them with more precise descriptions. A 30-up exercise is a fun and often challenging way to find new expressions for phrases you must use often or phrases you find repeated in your writing. Here's a 30-up exercise for the phrase *see the finish line,* which several early readers of this manuscript called to my attention.

Listening Exercises	other ways of saying "See the Finish Line"	by STEVE O'KEEFE
Payoff	Benefit	Result
Trophy	Prize	Parade
Improvement	New You	Change
The Reason	The Purpose	The Point
The Goal	The Objective	The Destination
The End of the Rainbow	The Checkered Flag	The Curtain Drop
Hear the Applause	Wear the Crown	Win the Title
Kick the Tires	See the Purse	Weigh the Cow
Weigh the Odds	Due Diligence	Squeeze the Produce

30-Up Cliché Buster for **See the Finish Line**

WRITING EXERCISE
CUSTOMIZING CLICHÉS

Take a favorite phrase or cliché and find as many different ways to say it as you can think of, up to a full page.

You get a better fix on your writing when you make clichés your own, by customizing them to the circumstances of *your* characters and *your* narrative. Once you get in the habit of circling clichés, they will light up on the page as if it's an illuminated treasure map. Many years ago I edited a manuscript written by a private investigator on the topic of using arrest records. Here are two sentences from that project: "You must always take these records with a grain of salt. They are by no means written in stone." Three clichés in nineteen words. Circle back on your clichés, dig a little deeper, and you will strike gold: an effective phrase for conveying an image with the fewest words possible.

CHAPTER 4

THINKING, TALKING, WRITING, READING

All writing originates in thought, so it's understandable that thinking and writing sometimes get confused. It is amazing how many people, myself included, think of the thought streams in our minds as "writing." That is a seduction to be avoided. I've spoken with dozens of people who want to be authors — and think they already are — because they have thoroughly worked-out streams of stories and articles in their heads. Until you translate those thoughts into words, you're not writing. You're thinking. They're two different things.

You cannot think your way through an entire novel, in advance, and just lay it down onto paper. Not even a single line is going to come out on the page the same way it sounds in your head. Something gets lost in translation. As soon as you render an idea in writing you'll see it's missing something: inflection, voice, nuance, shading, timing. Your thoughts are attached to emotions that somehow have to be reattached with alphabet. If you were speaking your thoughts, you could use tone of voice, gestures, and facial expressions to add this emotional depth to your words. As a writer, you have to find a way to fill that image out, restricting yourself to little smudges of contrast — letters and punctuation — the only tools you have to communicate *in writing*.

Thinking is a complex activity that is intermingled with the data we receive through our ears, eyes, skin, and so on. A great deal of thought is verbally expressed in the head: talking to yourself, thinking things through, planning, learning, reading. But this verbal self-talk is accompanied by emotional input that conditions everything the mind says to itself.

Without the ability to use our human voice and non-verbal communication to refine the meaning of our words, we must find a way to replace their nuance with vocabulary when we write. Writing is an extraction of the verbal component of thought. So is talking. But talking is accompanied by phrasing, eye movement, posture, and other nonverbal cues. A study of the meaning of spoken words conducted by Dr. Albert Mehrabian showed that 7 percent of the meaning came from the words themselves, 38 percent from tone of voice, and 55 percent from facial expression and physical movement. For our purposes, it's enough to say that talking and thinking are different, and both of them are different from writing.

Things don't sound the same when they come out in writing. You quickly find that you need to slow down and dig deep to come up with enough words to properly get across your meaning. This is why detail and clarity are praised so much in writing. In conversation, you must leave room to maneuver — to engage your partners in dialogue, to move the central focus along, to backtrack if necessary and take another run at a concept. Good conversation is organic and grows out of the mutual interests of those involved. In writing, it's you and the page, and the page contributes very little to the flow of thought. You can have a dialogue with yourself (see the section on Opposite Writing, page 91, for more on jump-starting your writing) or write for an imaginary reader, but you're still using your vocabulary and your ideas.

The mirror of writing is reading. Here we also have a verbal flow of ideas in the head, but the reader is mostly a passive recipient on the pathway of discovery. One writing instructor told me that out of speech, writing, and reading, speech required the least amount of vocabulary and reading the most. After all, you can't write words you've never heard, but you encounter them in reading all the time — and thrown together in ways that you might not be entirely comfortable with. The reader is always a little off balance, curiosity driving her forward to see where this will go next.

Research bears out these differences between speaking, writing, reading, and hearing. The average high school–educated English speaker has a spoken vocabulary of ten thousand words, can use forty thousand words when writing, and can recognize fifty thousand words when reading. These numbers are based on a massive sample size of two million test takers at TestYourVocabulary.com. When you use the exercises in this book to stimulate your written vocabulary, you supercharge your writing and make your writing time more productive.

Once you shift from thinking to writing, you can feel it at the keyboard. Your vocabulary puffs up like a peacock putting on a show. You find a rhythm as your staccato hunt-and-peck becomes a sewing machine stitching words and phrases together in sustained bursts, shaving seconds off the time it takes to write by sustaining the flow — and thereby saving hours and days off the time it takes to write a book.

Why Did Mrs. Montcrief Die?

Nothing kills a piece of writing faster than talking about it. We want to talk about our work so that we can think it through aloud, get insight from those we respect, and use that insight to refine our direction. However, more often than not, talking about writing substitutes for *actually writing* and kills off the desire to render that thought stream into writing. On this point, most of the arts agree: you can't talk your way through a painting, a piece of music, or a novel. Here is a lovely passage by the sculptor Henry Moore about the dangers of talking about your work: "It is a mistake for a sculptor or a painter to speak or write very often about his job. It releases tension needed for his work. By trying to express his aims with rounded-off exactness, he can easily become a theorist whose actual work is only a caged-in exposition of conceptions evolved in terms of logic and words."

I approach writers' workshops with extreme caution, because talking about my work or hearing others talk about it can ruin it for me. I look for an instructor who will give me compelling reasons to put words onto paper every week. I don't really want to get or give any feedback; I just want the word count and the practice.

The answer to almost all your questions about writing can be found through writing, not through talking or bashing or praising or debate. Almost all talk about writing will beat you into submission, sidetrack you, or, worst of all, stop the pleasant percussion of your keyboard in motion. Let me give a quick example.

In a writing class I took to help condition me for this book, one student answered the question, "What did you write about this week?" with the following tale. "I've been wanting to write about the adventures of Mrs. Montcrief, and I was telling my friends about the story and they didn't seem to think it was nearly as funny as I did. And I have to admit that it didn't sound as interesting when I was telling them about it, so I'm thinking I should write about something else — I'm not sure what." And just like that, the door to Mrs. Montcrief was shut — *without her ever having a chance to speak from the page.* No writing was performed that week — just talking — and that talking was a machine-gun staccato filling poor Mrs. Montcrief with terminal injuries. She died before she was born.

Why did Mrs. Montcrief die? Because when we talk about our work, we use only a fraction of the vocabulary we use when we write. We start developing Mrs. Montcrief on the spot rather than allowing her to develop at a more leisurely pace, in-depth, on the page. Of course, she seems small and weak — that's the language she's been given in speech. The wonderful woman in our heads, filled with the language of thought, emotions, and sensation becomes the shallow woman of speech. She sounds small even to the writer. If she were rendered in ink and alphabet, she might be a giant of a woman, deep, rich, hilarious. "Poor Mrs. Montcrief," this student said. Poor you, I thought. This is a painful lesson all writers have to learn: how to be excited about their work but to shut up about it, refusing to share it or talk about it until it is ready and until the receiver is someone they know to be encouraging.

Writing Is Discovery, Not Capture

Good writing is a process of discovery, not dictation. When you set the page on fire, you are anxious to see what comes next, and your readers catch fire as well. They can sense this unfolding and they, too, are anxious to see what comes next.

A lot of beginning writers think that writing a novel is a process of creating a plot and then fleshing it out with language. But for many professional writers, it doesn't work that way. Most of the novelists I have interviewed say it is more a process of listening to characters. You have these images of people in your head, and the images start walking and talking, and the writer tries his or her best to keep up and get it all down. In many cases, the writer is not conscious of where the story is going. He feels as if he is catching up with the story, not leading it. And that feel of the chase is transmitted to readers; if the writer is anxious to see what these characters will do next, most likely the reader will be, too. As author Jim Harrison put it, "Art should be a process of discovery, or it's boring."

You might have ideas for stories and articles in your

head, all neatly or not so neatly worked out, but when you go to put them on the page, something happens. The writing quickly heads in a direction of its own choosing.

Many writers feel as though they are being taken for a ride at the keyboard. You approach the page with one thought and, through the process of rendering it into words, you quickly move into feeling like a conduit rather than an originator. The writing moves through you. Your best writing will come as a surprise to you.

Good writing is as much a process of exploration as it is explanation. Thinking is good prep work — no writing happens without it — but unless those ideas get released through the writing process, they tend to go stale and rot. You can *see* this poem, this essay, this story, this book in your mind's eye, but you *can't* see what's waiting behind it — the words that need you to push that poem or essay or story out of the way so they can breathe.

Once you loosen the blockage by getting those ideas down on paper, new ideas begin to flow at a rate that will astound you, with clarity and detail that put your original concept to shame. At that point, you are traveling a road of discovery parallel to the reader's. The reader can feel that shift — longs for it — waits to be carried off by your crisp prose the way *you are* at the keyboard as the line of logic is revealed on the page.

Cultivating Your Dark Side

One reason would-be writers have trouble rendering their ideas into words is they are afraid of what they will uncover.

I was not prepared for this when I started teaching. My goal was just to get people writing. I believed that the answers to all questions about writing could be found by writing. You can talk and illustrate all you want, but no one will ever understand the writing process by trying to think it through. What I learned from teaching is that when people start writing, it doesn't take them very long to start writing about trauma.

Powerful writing is often distilled from powerful experiences. For better or worse, we tend to remember our hurts much more keenly than our pleasures. It doesn't take long in life to get hurt, and badly. Our culture doesn't encourage talking about those hurts unless it's on daytime television or with a professional therapist. When you combine a desire to write with serious pain that has gone unacknowledged or undiscussed, once you set the page on fire you will find yourself opening old wounds and examining them. I think a lot of potential writers realize this; pain drives some people away from writing for fear of what they might find.

Good writing comes from the clarity and intensity of the feelings we have about our traumas. It can be heartbreaking to read the prose of a mother whose child drowned, or a soldier who had no choice but to kill an enemy combatant — or who did have a choice and chose to kill. These are difficult events to live with, and they can be difficult to write about, too. However, once you set the page on fire, you'll see memories pour out of you with a fullness and detail you might never have experienced just thinking about them. Writing gets you to remember in ways that thinking does not. The writing mind can be quite detailed about things the thinking mind leaves vague and ill defined.

I am not a counselor, but I suspect this outpouring of old hurts is probably a good thing. Perhaps it enables writers to put their pain into context, or just put it in the past as something that *happened*, not something they're still going through. It might be that the only reason you're interested in writing is to get these episodes onto the page in the hopes of gaining a greater sense of understanding or some inner peace. Once you've written your way through them, it's possible that you will have gotten what you needed from the writing process.

A desire to deal adequately with tragedy is the motivating force behind about a quarter of the hundreds of writers I've interviewed. It's difficult to talk about hard things; it's easier to write about them. Writers say it takes only a few lines of type to return them to the time and the place of their tragedy; that's the power of this thing we call alphabet.

When I interviewed famous vampire novelist Poppy Z. Brite, I could not get a smile out of him, something I need from every interview for the still image we anchor the video to. I asked about his agent. Bad idea. I switched to his publisher. No kind words there. Finally, we started talking about restaurants in New Orleans, and he said the book gave him a chance to settle scores with all the bad places to eat in town. He smiled a devilish smile — the shot I needed — and went on to describe with great joy how much these restaurants fail. Writing from the dark side can lead to captivating prose because both writers and readers enjoy seeing justice prevail.

No amount of interviewing prepared me for the half

hour I spent with Joel Agee, son of the famous author James Agee. Joel's father died at the young age of forty-five on his way to the hospital. At the time, Joel was a child living in Berlin with his mother and his half-brother, Stefan. The following year, Joel's father posthumously won the Pulitzer Prize for Fiction for *A Death in the Family*, a novel based on the death of his own father, Joel's grandfather, in a car crash. Years later, as Stefan started slipping into madness, Joel got the idea that if he could reach his brother, he could pull him out of the darkness.

Joel used his writing to induce a mental illness similar to his brother's, an illness he almost did not escape from. He was unsuccessful in reaching his brother, who committed suicide. Joel himself was institutionalized and almost lost his own life. *In the House of My Fear: A Memoir* is the incredible story of this dark journey. You can watch my unsettling interview with Joel Agee at the companion website for this book.

Once you have dealt with your hurts as much as you feel you need to, you remove a blockage to all the other things you'd like to write about. In this sense, writing about the hurts can be a kind of exercise, in which you test how good you are at communicating strong feelings in prose (or poetry!). Don't be surprised if you find traumas bubbling up in your writing, even if you don't want to write about them or thought you were done with them. Writing is a process of discovery. Some of the things you discover will not be pleasant. Writer's block may be holding you back for good reason.

If you are an honest and persistent writer you will eventually uncover a dark side of yourself. What are you going to do with it? I think I know what Brenda Ueland would say: "Now we're getting somewhere! Get to know this charming devil — and take him around to the neighbors while you're at it." Just as I channel for Ueland, she channeled for William Blake, quoting him for one of the chapter titles in *If You Want to Write*: "Sooner strangle an infant in its cradle than nurse unacted desires." Yes, great horror fiction comes from looking in the mirror, our motivations often resembling the beasts we try to place ourselves above. Do you harbor nefarious desires? You may not be able to write your way around them. Once you find the dark side of your character, it will be difficult for you to write other material without first dealing with these demons.

Every Day Is Christmas Eve

One strategy for getting past writer's block is to go to the keyboard, accepting the fact that your first few paragraphs are likely to be lousy. Don't labor over them. Just like wrapping paper, they will be thrown away — the gift is what you'll keep. Let those first lines tumble out of you awkwardly and imperfectly, and let them go. You will quickly warm to the task, your pace will pick up, and you'll quietly become engrossed in what appears on the page as your writing voice surpasses the voice in your head that thought it could deliver a monologue.

As beautiful as that story is in your head, it's a thought form. It's not writing. The act of trying to put your thoughts into alphabet will change your thoughts. Once you go through the writer's warm-up and shift from your thinking brain into your writing brain, the process of writing will suggest avenues of expression that had never occurred to you. You'll find flaws in your characters you never knew existed. You knew exactly how your third act was going to unfold, but when you actually get there you find a new and more powerful third act, bittersweet and brilliant — where do you come up with this stuff?! From writing, of course, not from thinking. You find it while setting the page on fire.

The desire to write should make you feel as if it's Christmas Eve all the time. Your thoughts about the story or article you want to write are like glittering wrapping paper reflecting multicolored lights. Your plan for progressing through the material is like ribbon you have tied in your mind into a neat little bow. It's so exciting just to look at that present under the tree — what could be in there? To write is to start unwrapping the package at the keyboard. The gift itself is waiting just past paragraph three. You simply won't find out for sure what's in there until you open the package.

Your readers don't want to see only the wrapping of your piece — they want the gift, too. If you don't sit down to write, every day gets more and more frustrating. When can we open the presents? Writing is like having Christmas Eve every day — it's just that good!

CHAPTER 5

MAKING TIME TO WRITE

Lack of time is the most formidable barrier to writing. Where do you find the hours of quiet needed to compose a novel or write an article or draft a short story or create a poem? Okay, forget about the hours. Where do you find the twenty minutes required to pull out the notebooks and pens, open the computer files and find your place, then get through the writer's warm-up to where you're really saying something worth reading? It's hard to consistently find adequate chunks of time to accomplish something of value at the keyboard. How does one make time for writing?

"Quit wasting so much time sleeping" was one writing instructor's response to my complaints about not having enough time to write. I've met people who claim to sleep only three or four hours a night as a matter of routine, with no ill effects. I don't think that's a realistic strategy for solving the time problem for most writers. Writers have to steal writing time away from other claims, then defend it from attacks by friends, relatives, electronic devices, boredom, and

71

sloth. Following are a few techniques that might prove useful to you in creating and protecting your writing time.

How to Write a Book in Forty Hours

According to a massive survey of typing speeds conducted by TestYourVocabulary.com, the average high school graduate, native English speaker types English at forty words a minute. That's 2,400 words an hour. The average length of an English-language novel is 80,000 words. That means the average typist should be able to keyboard a novel in thirty-four hours. Do you still think you don't have enough time to squeeze writing into your life?

How many years do we walk around with stories or books in our heads, in our desk drawers, on our hard drives, unfinished, wishing we had time to write? Independent of all the thinking and research you do, the actual time spent keyboarding a manuscript is less than a forty-hour workweek. A handwritten manuscript of the same size can be completed in two forty-hour weeks. That amount of time should not be impossible to come by.

Writing and typing are not the same thing, you say. But yes, in fact, they are. Writing is the percentage of your thought that you have translated into alphabet, and nothing more. All the thinking about writing that you do — pondering what your characters would do in certain situations, researching the history of beekeeping, trying to get through that difficult scene that is not working — is lost except for that small portion that gets translated into alphabet and saved to the hard drive.

In order for your thoughts to appear between bound covers, someone needs to hit the keyboard about four hundred thousand times. And that should take less than forty hours of typing. So the first way to make time for writing is to spend less of your free time *thinking about writing* and more time *writing*: hitting the keyboard, scribbling words onto paper.

If you are anxious about finding the time to write a book-length manuscript, a personal memoir, or some other large project, try this: mark off a generous forty hours to render the book into written words, then jealously guard this time. You can pad that time with thinking or doing research, but make sure you get in forty hours — in the next six months or year — at the keyboard, and you will see a manuscript of some substance grow right under your fingertips. Some of the masterpieces completed in less than a month include *A Christmas Carol* by Charles Dickens, *A Clockwork Orange* by Anthony Burgess, *A Study in Scarlet* by Arthur Conan Doyle, and *The Prime of Miss Jean Brodie* by Muriel Spark.

When I wrote *Publicity on the Internet*, I completed the first two hundred pages in six months and the last two hundred pages in six weeks. While I was writing those last six chapters, I felt like the quality of the writing was dreadful. I would say to myself, "This is terrible. This is the worst writing I have ever done." But I just kept pounding it out, day after day, and you know what? The second half had a much stronger, more consistent voice. The second half was more cohesive than the first half. The writing lost accuracy but gained momentum. If you push yourself and stop fixing your writing as you go, you can produce a manuscript very quickly.

The Writer's Warm-Up

I first glimpsed the writer's warm-up in reaction to my own process at the typewriter. I came to the machine with a plan in mind: an idea and a desire to express it. I would begin to write and, if I was lucky, my fingers would start to get ahead of the plan and the page would catch fire. I would find the things that I *really* came to write about and burrow deeply into them. It's a stimulating and satisfying feeling, setting the page on fire. When you do, your reader will catch fire, too, and will follow as long as you burn.

Over the course of many years, I realized that the first few pages of whatever I had written — the planned part — could safely be discarded. The real energy was underneath. Try this in your own writing. Try to stay at it long enough in each session to get into that good groove where the words start lining up with remarkable precision and the vision gets acute. It is likely you will experience the phenomenon of the writer's warm-up.

The writer's warm-up is a transition period from a verbal stream of thought to a much faster written stream of thought. You begin by expressing something already contained in your mind in self-talk and quickly arrive at something you didn't know was there. You shift from explaining ideas to exploring them. The artist Paul Klee referred to this feeling as "taking a line for a walk." The wonderful thing about cultivating a regular writing practice is that the time it takes to get through the warm-up gradually diminishes. If you have been away from writing for a long time or are new to writing for pleasure, it might take you three pages to get rid of the ideas you came with and embrace the ideas you find. Within a matter of days, you will break through after three paragraphs. It's like one-two-three-write!

If you don't stay at the keyboard long enough each session, or you stay away from the keyboard for weeks at a time, it will take longer to generate that heat. Just like building a fire at a campsite, though, you will quickly remember how to arrange the "kindling" to get a good start. With a little practice, you will become an expert at finding the groove again. In her book *Conversations on Writing*, Ursula K. Le Guin wrote, "Getting started is hard. I throw away endless first pages grinding the gears until I can get the machinery going."

I saw in the works of dozens of students the same process I go through at the keyboard. Invariably, students begin with some general subject, such as romance or nature. Eventually the focus narrows to the author's personal experience of nature or romance. You begin by writing about the climate, and within a few paragraphs you are describing the cloak of humidity before yesterday's storm. When the writer hits his stride, the writing gets detailed, personal, valuable, real. It gains speed until it is moving like an express train carrying the reader along as the writer explores the terrain. Brenda Ueland says, "The secret of being interesting is to move along as fast as the mind of the reader can take it in."

I recently read an interview with prolific novelist M. J. Rose, who said that after three minutes at the keyboard she is locked in, writing as quickly as possible in an attempt to keep up with her characters. You can tell she writes every day. That's what happens when you cultivate the writing habit — you find yourself anxious to get to the keyboard or pad of paper and see what's inside you today, taking just a few moments to set the page on fire. One of the benefits of writing this way — openly, regularly — is that when you are consumed by your writing it's easy to lock out the distractions that would normally keep you from writing or annoy you when you do: music, the television, the air-conditioning, the kids.

Now that you know about the writer's warm-up, or have been reminded of the concept, see if you don't find it around you every day. I find it in newspaper articles all the time. Here's an example, an excerpt from a column in my local daily newspaper written by poet and writer Mary Lou Sanelli:

> There is so much to love about this lingering summer that, frankly, I don't know where to begin.
>
> The first thing I did when I moved to Port Townsend on a balmy summer evening over a decade ago was to drive to North Beach. With daylight still beaming at 9 PM, I headed for the sand to see the end of the day slip into the sea, sat on the fattest log until the sun, no longer round, sank below the horizon, its twilight making the rest of the sky seem even duskier.
>
> When warmth hovers into dusk, one rare pleasure — and to my mind the greatest pleasure — is

to eat dinner outside; best done when freshly mown grass swamps your toes and a cat sprawls on your heat-soaked deck. Tonight, engulfed by the wings of a dilapidated wicker arm chair, I do just that.

Do you feel the writer's warm-up here? Paragraph one: Mary Lou has just sat down to write. Her chosen topic is the long summer nights of August in the northern hemisphere. She is *thinking aloud*: "where to begin."

Paragraph two: Mary Lou is mining her memory which, as it is for most of us when we begin to write, is as hazy as the dwindling light. The cliché image of the sun sinking below the horizon is mitigated by its flattening — a unique expression.

Paragraph three: the writing deepens. The language gets richer with the warmth hovering into dusk. We smell the fresh-mown grass that cools her toes because, indeed, *Mary Lou has drilled down into the present moment*. By the time she reaches the wicker chair, she is in the moment and the page is on fire. From here out, the images are present, detailed, personalized, unique, and specific. The rest of this long summer evening is uniquely Mary Lou's.

WRITING EXERCISE
SPOTTING THE WARM-UP

Next time you pick up a newspaper or newsweekly, look for the writer's warm-up. It can be tricky to spot in a daily newspaper because journalists who write every day are perpetually warmed up. Also, many are aware of the writer's warm-up and guard against it, often by lopping off the first few lines of their work or having it cut by an editor. You're more likely to see the warm-up on the op-ed page or in longer feature articles.

When you spot the writer's warm-up — and you will, now that you know about it, for the rest of your life — cut it out and put it in your fake book or journal or file.

Puffensprachen

Eliminating the writer's warm-up is essential to the productivity of your writing practice and your happiness as a writer. When you set the page on fire, you write much faster. You enjoy the writing more because it is moving along at a pace you can barely sustain. You realize more output from your time at the keyboard, and that's satisfying, too, watching the word count ticking up.

Set the page on fire to become a happy, productive writer. You will save the time it takes to get through the writer's warm-up, which can be as long as twenty minutes. If you have only thirty minutes a day to write and the first twenty is taken up getting to the point where the writing is really sharp and original, you are going to quit writing. With a regular writing habit, twenty-nine of those thirty minutes are going to be productive and enjoyable. You bang out a lot more alphabet per hour when you set the page on fire.

When you write every day, you will be perpetually on fire. You will turn to-do lists into writing exercises. You will find yourself writing poems and book reviews and long emails and clever text messages. All of your writing will suddenly sparkle, because when you are in your writing brain, the right words come to you all the time.

One of the best ways to ignite the page is to start with a vocabulary exercise that forces you out of your verbal brain and into your writing brain in a few moments, often eliminating any warm-up period at the keyboard. My favorite vocabulary exercise is *puffensprachen*, a made-up word to describe the process of making up a new word at the beginning of a writing session to get into the writing mind. The trick is to create a word that contains several elements of what you are experiencing right now. If you're stretching out in the sun like a cat, you might be *felaxing*. Are you mad at the water company? You're in a *hydro-huff*. The words tend to sound a little German, piling one word on top of the next, but that's okay, that's *puffensprachen*!

> *Puffensprachen*: an exercise to puff up one's vocabulary by making up a new word and then defining it.

Every time I make up a new word, I feel like Bruce Banner becoming the Hulk as my vocabulary puffs up to four times its normal size before I take to the keyboard. Here's an example of a word many of my friends get a kick out of: *richtadichtaphobia*. It means an intense fear of the right lane. *Puffensprachen* pulls you through the writer's warm-up by forcing you to reach beyond the comforts of your speaking vocabulary into uncharted territory. One round of *puffensprachen* can save you fifteen minutes of warm-up.

I tried for years to get Stephen Colbert to use one of my

words for his "Word of the Day" segment, an audience favorite. I sent him *spindividualist* and *fecalnomics* and *suitsayer*, but he didn't use any of them. So today I have done my *puffensprachen* and my new word is *nobert*, meaning the inability to get your material onto Colbert.

Write a Little Every Day

Theoretically, if it takes forty hours to keyboard a manuscript, you could write a full-length book every year by spending only seven minutes a day at the keyboard. Realistically, writing doesn't work that way. I find I need a session of one to three hours long to accomplish something of value for the time spent writing. It's fairly easy to find five minutes every day for writing, but it can be a daunting task to consistently find a three-hour block of time. You have to secure a chunk of time that large every week if you want your writing to accumulate into publishable pieces. When I'm writing a book, I need a block of one to three hours at least five days a week to sustain the flow. For articles, I need just one chunk a week. For short stories, two.

One of the problems with scheduling your time at the keyboard is getting your muse to show up between 1:00 and 3:00 PM on Saturday afternoon. You're holed up in the basement, ready to produce the next five thousand words, and your muse is at the beach with the kids, relaxing in the hot summer sun. What can you do?

Train your muse.

You can teach your muse to show up at the appointed time by having at least a brief conversation with him or her every day. We've learned about the writer's warm-up and how if you have a limited schedule for writing, this warm-up will eat you up. Just knowing you face this relatively unproductive time at the keyboard places a psychological barrier to getting started. If you don't get started, the writing never adds up. Your muse gets farther and farther away the less you need him or her. When you finally overcome that barrier and get started, you have to put in a missing person's report to find your muse.

Writing — that is, typing or taking pen to paper — is the way you call your muse. You don't want to have to call long-distance. When you write a little every day, your muse stays in the local dialing zone — within earshot, even — waiting to hear the clack of the keys or the scratch of the nib, anxious to find out what you're writing about today.

If you write a little every day, your thinking voice and your writing voice are in sync, like a mathematical equation and its derivative, like parallel curves that rise and fall in unison, like synchronized swimmers. When you write a little every day, your muse can show up halfway through the first sentence, looking over your shoulder to see what you are writing, then whispering suggestions into your ear. You call your muse with the sounds of writing, and you keep the muse close by calling on him or her every day.

Once your muse has been properly trained to respond to the sound of the keyboard or to the scratching of the pen on paper, you can have a productive writing session in as little as fifteen minutes. Journals are

> You call your muse with the sounds of writing, and you keep the muse close by calling him or her every day.

a great way to keep the muse close at hand between longer writing sessions. If you write a little every day, you won't lose the first twenty minutes when you have only one long writing block a week. Letters work well, too — not just notes but real letters, thoughtful and meaty. Book reviews make terrific interim writing projects; they help you fix a book in your memory. Even transcribing your favorite passages out of a book and into your fake book qualifies as checking in with the muse, who will hear you writing and come running to see what you are working on.

Writing every day also helps you cultivate the writing habit, weaving it into your routine between morning cups of coffee, or into the half hour of the day when the children are not underfoot, or into the half hour before you retire for the night. Even if you're only writing snippets a day, they will add up, and when your schedule allows blocks of one to three hours for serious writing, you'll have an irreplaceable treasure box of material that can instantly transport you to a place and a time as though it were yesterday and just around the corner.

Night Writing

One of the things that stood out from the AuthorViews interviews is the large percentage of authors who write in the middle of the night. Elaine Viets, author of the Dead-End Job Mystery series, told me she writes from 3:00 to 6:00 AM every day. She blames her writing schedule on the lack of affordable day care. Working a series of "bottom-rung-of-the-ladder" jobs left her with little money or time. But it also led to a great basis for a fiction series — fifteen volumes and going strong — each involving a murder discovered by the lowest person on the payroll.

US Civil War historian Will Hutchison does all his writing after midnight. The author of *Follow Me to Glory*, he literally followed in the footsteps of his main character, General Scott, by walking the exact routes Scott and his troops traveled. Mike Maranhas, author of the novel *Re'enev*, writes from 3:00 to 5:00 AM every day before going to work. Many authors find the quiet they need to create when the world around them sleeps. You might give night writing a try if you haven't already. Here are some suggestions to get you started:

- If you can't sleep one night, try to get a few paragraphs of writing in. If you like how it went, try building it up a few minutes each night until you get to one hour.
- Take a nap after dinner and get up at 10:00 PM to do your writing. I stayed on that schedule for a couple of years.
- Try getting up one hour before anyone else in the household, and use that hour to write.
- Most of the night writers I've interviewed write their first drafts in longhand so as not to disturb the quiet they like to write in.

One of the surprises I discovered from interviewing novelists is that many consciously try to use their dreams to advance their writing. One way is to instruct yourself, before you go to sleep, on what you hope to accomplish, such as the next scene, the next chapter, or a passage you're struggling with. You wake up in the morning and immediately write down what you experienced in the night. For some authors, the writing is like transcription, in which they capture a voice that is dictating to them. Others don't program their dreams but do immediately write them down in the morning. Some find the material they need coming through those dreams. Using your dreams to advance your writing is a clever way of getting around time commitments.

WRITING EXERCISE
WRITE DOWN YOUR DREAMS

Try recording your dreams in a journal. You will remember them most strongly in the morning. However, you'll find that writing down last night's dreams just before bed tonight will lead to dreams extending across multiple nights or "episodes." Stop if it's not working for you.

WRITING EXERCISE
PROGRAM YOUR DREAMS

Before retiring for the night, instruct yourself as to what you would like to dream about. Keep the instructions loose, such as "What should I do with this character?" or "What should I write about tomorrow?" Try to write down the resulting dreams, even if at first you don't think they relate. See if you can get the instructions and the dreams to start correlating. Stop if it's not working for you.

Dreams are really strange, and I should add a caveat, like a yoga instructor, not to do any exercises beyond your comfort zone. The great psychologist Carl Jung recorded his dreams to the point of near madness. The result is one of the most famous dream journals of all time, *The Red Book*, a gigantic illuminated guide to the inner workings of the mind. I've kept dream journals on and off, but I had a bad experience once. After six months of nightly journaling, I decided I didn't want to do it anymore, but I couldn't turn off the dreams. It took months to get back to my usual zombie sleep after which I remember few dreams, and those only vaguely.

Writing as Stand-Up

One way many professional writers make time for writing is by thinking of their writing as a gig, a performance, a stand-up routine, or a show. In this way, they have a schedule, and meeting that schedule leads to completing the writing.

The bestselling writer in Canada is children's author Robert Munch. His written stories start out as verbal tales shared with children in classroom visits. He adjusts every word and phrase based on audience response. It sometimes takes years of development before he is ready to write down one of his stories. In an interview, Munch told me he likes working in front of children because they get bored very quickly. If the material doesn't hold their attention, they won't be polite about it.

Writing this way is not the same as basing your writing

on verbal language; the language is based on what works live. That's very different from natural speaking, which would result in nap time or revolt if practiced on a room full of first graders. Munch's writing is strategic, planned, refined. He puts the gestures and intonation back into the words. Comedy writers work long hours to make their jokes sound natural; the jokes don't just come out of their mouths that way. The lines in a David Mamet play sound like nothing real people have ever said to each other; they are much more sublime than that. They've been written to be sharp and re-written to be smooth.

The crucial aspect of writing as stand-up is the schedule you keep. If you have problems committing to an hour of writing every night, consider turning your writing time into a live, streaming show: *The Writer Show.* Put yourself in front of the keyboard, place your camera phone so people can see you typing, and livestream it on Facebook Live or YouTube or Twitch or Vimeo — or whatever platform you prefer.

As I write this, several people are live-streaming themselves studying on YouTube. They are sitting at their desks, reading and taking notes. It has become popular in many colleges and universities to relieve the tedium of studying by studying "with" someone online. Some people are able to earn money online by letting people watch them study, watch them exercise, or watch them eat. You could turn your writing time into a revenue stream! Seriously, I would pay a buck or two just to watch my favorite writers sitting at the computer, spanking the alphabet.

WRITING EXERCISE
COMEDY ROUTINE

Turn your writing assignment into a routine, and improve the writing by improving the routine. Try writing a business plan as ten short jokes, or a short story as one long joke, or a piece of dialogue as a comedy routine, or a chapter as a sketch comedy.

Airplane Mode

If writers were as inventive with their fictional characters as they are with making excuses for not writing, we would be deep into the greatest literary renaissance of all time. To write, you need only one of the following two things:

1. A light surface and a dark marker
2. A dark surface and a light marker

Writing is contrast. Don't complicate it.

You don't need a computer to write a book. You can write longhand or shorthand or on a typewriter, or you can dictate a book. As you know, I have worked with several blind high school students on recording their thoughts using voice transcription software and building up substantial written pieces, which they edit by hearing the computer read it back aloud, paragraph by paragraph. It's a fascinating process of transforming ideas into sounds into letters and then back into sounds in a different voice so you can hear the problems!

Many successful writers write entire manuscripts in longhand. Then they edit the first draft by hand and keyboard the edited draft or have an assistant keyboard it. I write with a typewriter, edit the first draft by hand, then keyboard the edited draft into Microsoft Word or Google Docs or ZohoWriter. One way or another, most long works end up on the computer for editing and publishing. However, using a computer to write the first draft can prove detrimental to actually finishing a book.

Writing on the computer comes with a major distraction: the tendency to edit while you write. You can click into an electronic thesaurus to find better words. You can easily erase or move sentences. Formatting wants to be done as you type: italics, bold, indents, bulleted lists, section headers and subheads, style sheets, page headers and footers, index markers....Fussing with format can easily derail your train of thought. Most successful writers recommend burning through the rough draft just about as fast as you can type. Don't worry about editing until later.

When that computer is hooked up to the internet, you keyboard in a very noisy environment. You have the easy lure of email to pull you away from your train of thought. Then there's the ever-present web, containing everything you ever wanted to know about anything but extracting a time toll in your attempt to locate it. During one session at the typewriter, I wrote that Katherine Anne Porter won the National Book Award. Or was that a Pulitzer? If I were writing on a computer, I would have googled her name to fact-check the award, quickly finding a bio of Porter and getting pulled in. Did you know she married four times? She lived in New Orleans for a while — one of my hometowns — and wrote her stories at the Pontalba Building overlooking Jackson Square. Look, here's a picture of her with Eudora Welty. And here's a link to a site on Welty....Two hours later, you window back to Word and shut down the machine. Well done! For your 150 minutes at the keyboard you have ten minutes of meandering warm-up and one solid fact about Katherine Anne Porter. Better luck tomorrow.

When I'm at my laptop, I'm all business. My language changes from luxurious and relaxed to abrupt, functional, and brittle. I have such a hard time crafting sensitive prose on the computer that I keep an old Underwood Champion manual nearby for rough drafts. I write about fifty news releases a year for book publishers. Most of my clients aren't aware of this, but the first draft is always done longhand or on the typewriter. I use the computer for research and editing, spell-checking and formatting, correspondence and publishing, but seldom for real writing.

For those who have had trouble getting enough satisfying writing out of the computer, try typing while offline — no email or web browsing — and try to write first and format later, when you edit the first draft. I think you'll be surprised by how much your productivity goes up when you write in stages like that, disconnecting from the grid for the rough draft and using the full arsenal of word processing, page layout, and the world wide web to build out and buff the second draft.

In Praise of Typewriters

Over many drafts of the manuscript that became *Set the Page on Fire*, numerous advance readers have added margin notes that are variations of "You don't really type on a typewriter, do you?" and "You mean *keyboard*, not *typewriter*, right?" No. I mean typewriter. To be specific, I mean a manual typewriter: no cord, no battery. Muscle powered. It marks the end of the analog era: a keyboard that works anywhere and stores nothing.

You'll notice that writing with a manual typewriter is *not* one of the top secrets of successful writers. I'm not recommending it. But now that it's out there, I want to share how much I love writing on a manual typewriter. Every single letter of the rough draft for this book was carved with machine steel into heavy cotton bond before being keyboarded into a computer. In one of the great ironies of a long writing career, I wrote the first draft of *Publicity on the Internet* in 1996 on a manual typewriter. Why in the world would I do such a thing?

First, habit. A manual typewriter was my most prized possession as a child. Second, speed. I type about sixty words a minute, slightly faster than I can think. Third, piano. I'm an amateur pianist, and using a manual typewriter helps build finger strength and reduce repetitive stress injuries. Fourth, the sound. The percussion is loud enough to let everyone within a quarter mile know I'm composing and to leave me alone. Fifth, the quiet. When I pause to think, there is absolute silence. There is nothing you can do with a typewriter except write.

Writing on a manual typewriter is basically the same as writing longhand in that both are original drafts that are then edited and keyboarded. The difference is that typing is much faster. I still do a lot of original writing in longhand, like many professional writers, but it's slow going at twenty words a minute. I feel like I'm always waiting for my hand to catch up. When I type sixty words a minute, it feels like a thinking pace.

At one time, manual typewriters were a major engine of the American economy. Millions were turned out every year, and thousands of people were employed in typewriter factories in places such as Dayton, Ohio. Typewriter design is a human achievement, their dished keypads begging to be touched, their raised tiers that allow rapid typing without key collision. You press a key and it presses back, springing to life at your touch. Each sheet of paper is fed by hand and carries your prints, your oils into the machine, where it will be tattooed by hand, carved and inked and left to dry.

I enjoy cleaning and aligning manual typewriters as a form of meditation. Too much time alone with my typewriter led to the following technique, "opposite writing," in which you simply divide your own personality, Hydra-like, to achieve different characters or points of view.

Opposite Writing

One way to get around writer's block is to write the opposite of whatever you think you should be writing. Is your leading man a fast-thinking dynamo of few words with rippling muscles? Let's age him, put him in adult diapers, and have everyone else in the story say, "What's that smell?" whenever he passes. Have you been assigned to write the piece "Five

Simple Things to Help Sell Your House Quickly"? Try writing five simple things you can do to ensure that your house stays on the market for eighteen months and sells at half the asking price.

Opposite writing has a long history, dating back to at least Socrates. The pathway to knowledge was thought to go through adversity. For an idea to be accepted as true, the opposite had to be false. Testing an idea against every conceivable alternative is the concept behind Plato's *Dialogues,* the result of a writer having a dialogue with himself. Opposite writing peaked with René Descartes, the French philosopher whose motto was "Question everything."

I started using opposite writing in college with a two-color typewriter ribbon: red and black. I would type a statement in black, then question it in red, then respond in black, and so on. It's helpful for writing dialogue. It helps with finding new ways of expressing common sentiments. More than anything, it helped me get started. Type whatever comes to mind, then challenge it. Just like that, you're into your writing mind. Try it. The following contrarian exercise is liberating. It helps you loosen up and have fun at the keyboard. Fairly quickly, the words will start lining up in a pleasing arrangement that satisfies both writer and reader.

 WRITING EXERCISE
THE ZIPPER

Write down a statement on a sheet of paper (or on your phone, tablet, computer — anything handy). Then write the exact opposite of that statement. Using two different colors or fonts enhances this exercise, because the idea is to develop two contrary voices. Continue going back and forth between these two contrary sides until you get bored, usually a few minutes. Did the zipper help you get started? Did it lead to useful insights in the development of your article, story, or characters?

Opposite writing led to one of the best article placements I've had in a long writing career. I put a case history of a botched book PR campaign on my website. It quickly became the most popular page on my site. So I put up another. My traffic soared. Kristen Clarke, editor of *Associations Now* magazine, noticed the case histories and asked for an article about failure. Surely, I thought, there is no one more qualified to do this assignment! The final article was called "Lessons in Failure" and ran in *Associations Now,* which has a readership of forty thousand association executives. I was paid, got a byline, and picked up several new customers.

Another effective way to smash through writer's block is to start in the middle. If you're working yourself up to a torrid love affair, start with the sex and backfill the story. If there is a dramatic climax to your novel, write that first. Have you noticed how many screenplays do that? They start on what was page 480 of the original book, then go back to the beginning. Are you afraid of giving away the ending? That's what we do as writers — we give away the story. By giving it away you get it out of the way so you're free to write the rest. Try to begin at the most fascinating point, and don't worry that the reader hasn't been properly prepared.

CHAPTER 6

EASY OUTLETS FOR YOUR WRITING

Most writers need to feel like they are writing *to someone* or *for someone* in order to gather the momentum to work diligently through a piece of prose. Here are some suggestions for ways to tap your writing powers in ordinary life.

Journaling

Journal writing is a popular way to keep your muse close between substantial writing sessions and to accumulate content you can develop through those sessions. You may have difficulty imagining your journals adding up to anything. However, if you begin writing short stories and articles, you'll find ideas and characters first discovered in your journals percolating up into your longer pieces. Knowing that there is an audience for material in your journals will hopefully make you feel more comfortable writing a little every day, confident that you are unearthing good things that you may someday be able to share with others.

This process — discovery through journal writing and refinement through longer writing sessions — goes on whether or not you realize it. I seldom read back through my journals looking for content to develop. I may someday, but for now that writing is water under the bridge. My journal is the bridge, the vantage point from which I sketch the picture of life going by. Several of the authors I have interviewed expressed the same sentiment: they keep journals because the ideas expressed in them eventually inform their work.

One of my writing instructors recommended the work of Katherine Anne Porter, and after class I stopped at a used book store to see if I could sample her on the cheap. I didn't find any of her books, but there was a collection of her letters. After a long hiatus from publishing, Porter won the National Book Award and the Pulitzer Prize. Her only novel, *Ship of Fools*, was based on a journal she kept during a long cruise some thirty years earlier. That gave me more confidence in what other authors have repeatedly told me — that my journals will be a valuable source of story ideas and content someday.

Journaling can get out of hand. Remember when I recommended that you keep a Fake Book of Favorite Quotations? Other than that, try to write a little every day, whether in journals, diaries, letters, emails, blogs, or notes to yourself. For many years my journal was a cardboard box into which I tossed the output from sessions at the typewriter. If I had a poetry reading pending or had promised someone an article or story, I would rifle through the box and find an idea to develop. Simple. You don't have to call it a "journal," and it doesn't have to be in a bound book or a phone app. The important thing is to write.

Dr. Tel Franklin wrote a book called *Expect a Miracle* about "appreciative medicine," built around the practice of medical journaling. Patients start a medical journal under the supervision of a trusted health care provider, then share this journal periodically with all their medical providers. The journal contains entries on such things as what symptoms they are experiencing, how they reacted to various medicines or procedures, and how they see their health one or two years from now.

The positive results of medical journaling reported by Dr. Franklin are sometimes spectacular and come from anecdotal evidence provided by patients themselves — through their journals. Patients felt more in charge of their treatment and, consequently, took charge of their health. What I found most intriguing were the studies indicating that the process of journaling is in itself therapeutic. That is, the act of journaling reduces heart rate, respiration rate, and anxiety, which in turn increases the efficacy of prescribed treatments. If you don't yet have enough reasons to keep some sort of journal, add this item to your list: it's good for your heart.

Correspondence

When was the last time you sat down and wrote a letter that was more than two paragraphs long? The art of the personal letter has all but disappeared. I thought email would herald the return of the personal letter, but it was quickly replaced by text messaging and now by emoji. The few corresponding buddies I had mostly switched over to email, then switched off. I continue to send a steady dose of rambling paper-and-stamp letters, but I rarely receive anything in return. I have lost the benefit of hearing regularly from some of my favorite writers. This is a great loss indeed.

Have you ever had a letter battle with someone? Do you have a correspondent who has been able to write once a week steadily for months? A robust correspondence is one of the greatest delights of being human. You come home after work wondering if there will be a new missive in the mailbox, speculating on how your correspondence partner might have replied to your last retort. Then one day you find a letter and set it next to your easy chair. Later that night you slice it open and hastily read through it to find — egads! – there's no mention of you! Not one word about your last letter! Fool! Then you read it again, more slowly this time, to find out what's on his mind. And in the following days, as you perform your ablutions at the bathroom sink, you ponder how to respond to this latest salvo. Letters, like journals, can help you work through ideas, fix images in your mind, and find characters to populate your stories.

A robust correspondence is one of the greatest delights of being human.

I've enjoyed a few epic correspondences in my lifetime. In college my buddy and I had a twice-a-week letter exchange that ran for a few years, mostly concerning philosophical matters: testy dissertations on religion, science, and the nature of reality. We still write to each other, but it's more like twice a year now. A college friend who lives in Alaska has been an off-and-on correspondent for the past three decades. At one point we exchanged a series of amateur naturalist letters at a pace of about one a week, with him describing the rugged beauty of Alaska in great detail and me describing the sultry swamps of City Park in New Orleans. I also had a vigorous exchange with Canadian musician and author Kenneth Maue for the better part of two years.

Letter exchanges can be vital; good writing pours through them, and writing them keeps your muse close. But they're also fleeting. They have a place and a time, and it's better to remember them fondly for what they were than to mourn their loss and stop writing. I urge you to keep trying to find an interesting correspondent to swap letters with. You will never lack for an audience and are apt to keep writing. And correspondents can provide valuable insight into problems you are trying to work out at the keyboard — observations that you, as author, are sometimes too close to make.

Most of the published authors I interviewed for this book brought up the subject of correspondence with fans as one of the most rewarding yet time-consuming aspects of being a popular writer. Many successful authors spend hours every afternoon responding to fan mail. Responses from readers are what first-time authors mention first as the most rewarding result of getting published. Communications from readers often are the basis of sequels. In the case of the Chicken Soup for the Soul series, almost the entire series came from readers sending in their own stories. Famous writers often have their best letters published. New World Library, my publisher, just released a wonderful collection of letters by Alan Watts and sixty years of correspondence by Joseph Campbell. Your investment of time in correspondence can result in new ideas, collaborations, material for larger manuscripts, and, someday, possibly collections of your own letters.

The Great Postcard Exchange

My brother, Kelly O'Keefe, is not much of a writer. There's nothing wrong with his writing — after all, we are all talented, original, and have something important to say. He's more of a visual communicator. A trained and talented artist, he often sends me drawings he made while on vacation instead of letters. That works. There are nine muses, you'll recall, and time spent with any one of them — playing music, dancing, acting, singing — helps keep the whole muse family nearby. Drawing is not the same as writing, but the creative arts inform one another, and the crossover helps you set the page on fire.

One day I found a homemade postcard in the mail, sent by Kelly. The next day I received another. "Interesting," I thought. The next day another card arrived. "What's he up to?" I wondered. Then another. "All right," I thought, "two can play this game." I started sending postcards back, at first with routine information about family, work, and weather, and then slowly catching fire and becoming more creative with vignettes, character studies, and profound observations. And so the Great Postcard Exchange was born.

 OUR HOLIDAYS WERE A WONDERFUL TIME FOR ALL OF US. WE ATE OUR FEAST OF FRUIT & CANDY, RAVIOLI AND PISTACHIO NUTS. WE PLAYED WITH NEW TOYS, READ NEW VOLUMES AND PAINTED WITH NEW BRUSHES. OUR HOME, FILLED WITH CAROLS AND COLORED LIGHTS BECAME STREWN WITH BOWS AND COLORED PAPERS. WE THANK YOU FOR YOUR GIFTS WHICH WERE SO MUCH A PART OF THIS FESTIVE HOLIDAY.

Steve, Storme & Franceska O'Keefe
H Street
Port Townsend, WA.
98368

One of the hundreds of postcards sent during the Great Postcard Exchange (used with permission of the artist, Kelly O'Keefe)

Four or five postcards traversed each direction every week. As the battle wore on, I consumed every four-by-six-inch surface in the house. I began cutting up cereal boxes, candy boxes — any kind of packaging material that was blank on one side. Kelly was doing likewise. As the weeks rolled into months, we tested the patience of the postal authorities: a piece of automotive grillwork he sent with paper glued to one side made it through; a banana I wrote on and applied adequate postage to did not. The battle raged for about six months. Entire short stories were written in three-paragraph increments. Artwork was created. Thoughts were refined. Then the pace of exchange slowed until about two years later it was over, played out, put to rest.

While the Great Postcard Exchange was raging, it was fun for everyone involved. Our spouses and children would look over the new arrivals and make comments and suggestions, but I don't recall any of them entering the fray. A little corner of my brain was perpetually on fire, thinking through the three paragraphs I would launch that day, rummaging through the garbage in search of more canvases for my prose. And Kelly was on fire at the other end of the swap, looking for ways to outdo his previous masterpieces. Our postal carriers became characters in the drama as we started writing to them, knowing none of our correspondence was private — surely we had gotten their attention by now.

Around the same time, the book *Griffin & Sabine* came out, to critical acclaim and sales success. People who heard about my postcard exchange with Kelly kept saying, "You should check out *Griffin & Sabine* — it's a postcard exchange between lovers." So I did check it out, of course, but I didn't buy it. What a letdown. The exchange never happened. The postcards are fabricated. The writing is great — don't get me wrong — I applaud anyone's attempt to render the world in words. But for me it was a great disappointment to see this bestselling fiction when my brother and I had the real deal going.

> I applaud anyone's attempt to render the world in words.

Today I have his half of the Great Postcard Exchange in a file box in storage, and he has my half tucked away somewhere. I am looking forward to the day when we unite the two halves of the collection for the first time and put the cards back into order, reliving one of the most enjoyable writing projects of my life. Don't deny yourself the pleasures of writing a long letter or engaging in a postcard battle; it will do wonders for keeping your muse close and providing ideas and language for longer pieces of writing.

Blogging

Blogging is an excellent way to publish short fiction and non-fiction and watch it accumulate into book-length works. The word *blog* is short for *web log*, a form of diary software incorporated into many online systems. Facebook feeds are blogs, Twitter is a microblogging platform, and LinkedIn now offers blogs. Anyone can start a blog for free at Blogger, Word-Press, Goodreads, and many other sites. Amazon doesn't yet offer blogs, but if you have a blog, you can attach it to your

Amazon Author Central page, and your posts will automatically appear on Amazon.

Blogging used to be a good way to make a living as a freelance writer. So good that in 2010 I partnered with David Reich to start SixEstate, offering a new kind of journalism we called "newsblogging." We hired dozens of writers from throughout the United States to write daily blog posts on subjects they were experts in. Businesses and nonprofit organizations would come to us to get blogs on their websites so they could rank higher in search engines. SixEstate would hire the writer, attach him or her to an editor, assign topics, add design and art to finished pieces, and manage the publication platform.

SixEstate has writers in travel, business, law, medicine, architecture, biology, childhood education, LGTBQ rights, women's issues, veterans' issues, poverty, publishing. I spent years with a team of writers and editors there developing writer's guidelines and editor's guidelines, our rulebooks. The experience soured me on writer's guidelines. They are outdated the moment they are completed and siphon energy from actually practicing journalism. If you're an expert at anything, and you like to write, blogging is still a great way to earn some money, build up byline credits, and gain visibility. Look for a company you admire that could use a better blog, and pitch yourself as a blogger.

Blogging is a good side gig, but it's a tough way to make a living. Our professional blogging teams were increasingly pitted against amateur bloggers who blog for free in exchange for a byline and a link. If you pay writers a living wage, over time you lose accounts to free bloggers. In several cases, our blogs were so successful that our clients built the same editorial team in-house. If you are an outside service, you are always subject to termination at will. SixEstate survived by broadening its services to include pushing blog posts to third-party sites. In essence, the same clients now pay to have the same blog posts put on other people's websites instead of their own.

Over time, SixEstate expanded the writer pool to include English-language writers anywhere in the world. We used sites such as Guru and UpWork and TaskRabbit to find writers with verifiable college degrees and journalism experience. What attracted us to certain writers was their ability to deliver something we could work with, despite all obstacles. The mechanics were not as important to us as reliability. We had in-house editors who could fix anything. For many of our authors, English was a second language, and our editors translated the articles into American English. So don't let poor mechanics or lack of fluency in a language stop you from writing!

When we started out, we could get as much as $250 for a blog post written by a celebrity writer. In 2015, when I left the business to focus on authors and books, we could get $50, tops. After you pay an editor, a graphic artist, and a search engine expert to groom the post, there's not much left over for the writer. One of the last projects I worked on at SixEstate involved teaching an artificial intelligence system how to produce a top-ranking blog. An increasing amount of content is being machine written, cutting deeper into writer pay scales. Today it's best to think of blogging as a great way to build a portfolio and a following but not a nest egg.

In 2005 my brother, Virginia Commonwealth University Brandcenter professor Kelly O'Keefe — he of the Great Postcard Exchange — started a family blog on BlogSpot. He has four sons, all visual artists, and it became a place to share work. Thanks to Hurricane Katrina, I was a guest at my brother and sister-in-law Cristy's home in Richmond, Virginia, for a few months in 2005. I was let in on the family blog, named *Cardboard Rhino*. It is full of art, stories, crafts, and even music, all handmade by the contributors to the blog, a font of creativity documenting the rise of a unique family ability for drawing comics. Work on the *Cardboard Rhino* has led directly or indirectly to commercial publication, grants, and teaching positions for my nephews, who built substantial portfolios at the site.

Cardboard Rhino had a good ten-year run (and is still open to the public at Cardboardrhino.blogspot.com), but as the boys aged from teens into adults and started families of their own, the posts trailed off. If you find an outlet like this for your personal work, it will help you keep the rhythm of writing when the commercial markets or the weather turns against you.

Business Communications

One way to make time for your writing is to steal it from your employer. Employee theft has doubtless launched more periodicals than Condé Nast. It is a common path for undiscovered writers holding down McJobs to pilfer the storeroom for supplies, use the company copier to propagate their work, and run a tab up on the postage meter without telling anyone or settling up. As an employer myself, I'm not sure I want to encourage such behavior. The kind of theft I'm interested in fostering is different — it's more expropriation than outright robbery.

The theft I'm talking about is time — the time it takes to turn a piece of business correspondence into a work of art. Many jobs require that you write something every day. It might be an email order confirmation, a systems analyst's report, a shopping list, an invoice, a Post-it note, a collection letter, financial statements, phone messages, or myriad other combinations of numbers and letters that lubricate the gears of commerce. What I'm asking you to do is, maybe once a month, to take one of those routine assignments and play with it a while, creatively, with the goal of communicating with sharper clarity and originality — or just of having some fun at no one's expense. By taking a few precious moments of your employer's time to break out of the cubicle of corporate communications, you can learn how to check in with your muse at work. Then this muse will start coming to work with you more regularly, and your employer will most likely be delighted at the ingenuity of your written communications. That's the kind of employee theft I heartily endorse!

How many times do you really try to communicate gracefully in the mundane documents of commerce? My email writing style is so functional that any attempt to be intuitive or poetic takes a true act of will. When I see beauty in my own emails, it's startling, because it's so rare. When I see it in the emails of others, it's refreshing.

My friend, e-commerce guru Ken McCarthy, has written some of the most thoughtful, effective emails I've ever received. Ken truncates his emails at about twenty or thirty characters per line. I asked him about this once and discovered that he never changed the settings in his email software — he hits the return key as he writes, visually breaking the line where it feels natural. The result is emails with natural phrasing and a visual presentation similar to poetry — except the messages are not all polished up like a poem. His emails read just like well-phrased business letters. They communicate economically and elegantly. No wonder people turn to Ken for advice on copywriting for electronic media.

Are you warming to this idea yet? Imagine if the phone messages we took down *really* communicated what transpired. Instead of "Call Mary Collins," you could find a note one day that says, "Mary Collins phoned at 3:12 today. She seemed surprised you weren't here, though she didn't have an appointment. Her voice sounded urgent, pulled through the fuzz box of a cell phone, fading in and out like a distant AM radio station on a moonless night. She'd like you to call her when you get in." Okay, so it's not Hemingway, and the boss might think you've gone off your nut. And it could get irritating and cliché, getting messages like that every day. But once in a while it's charming. It wakes you up to the potential to turn anything into a productive writing exercise. And it wakes the boss up, too. Maybe she'll start asking you to help write her speeches instead of taking phone messages all day!

If you are in a position to modify your business communications for the greater glory of the divine word, you will find that the attempt is entertaining and has long-term benefits. One Office Depot list written in the worshipful language that office supplies deserve, one dun letter that attempts to sympathize with the financial straits of the deadbeat at the other end, one news release that acknowledges that the reader is a human being who has been punched with blunt pitches fifty times already today, one purchase order that contains a handwritten, heartfelt note of thanks for a supplier's past performance, one honest billing log that identifies which of the minutes were most effective and which the least — these are the small things that soften the sharp edges of commerce. They can make both sender and receiver feel more alive, more human, while opening your eyes to the limitless writing opportunities all around you. Anyone care to join me for Take Your Muse to Work Day?

Reviews

Reviews are the best thing about being a writer. If you can write, you can review. If you can review, you can be heard.

As I've mentioned, I am a volunteer technology coach at the Virginia School for the Deaf and the Blind. One of the great motivators for students learning how to write is the ability to review music and videos on YouTube. Kids will jump over almost any barrier if they believe the end result will be their opinions being showcased on YouTube. They cannot wait to tell the world what they think about the lack of accessibility in their lives. They want to review their cell phones, their favorite videos, their favorite music, and their favorite tech. Reviewing is a way of breaking out of the small world that many special needs kids find themselves in.

Reviewing books is an excellent way for a writer to break into any publication. Reviews are welcome on most special-interest websites. Reviews generate revenue for popular sites through advertising and bookstore affiliate revenue. If you see that a favorite website uses an affiliate bookstore to generate revenue, that's a good potential outlet to pitch book reviews to.

Amazon is a great place to place book reviews, as long as you haven't transferred the rights to another publication. Thoughtful Amazon reviews come to the attention of the book's author, editor, and agent. These people will be more receptive to pitches from you if they have already seen your reviews on Amazon. You can gain visibility for your Amazon reviews by publicizing them. Amazon assigns a unique URL to each review, and the more traffic your review receives, the higher it ranks in Amazon's algorithm. Your Amazon reviews will drive people to your Amazon profile, where, as mentioned above, you can attach your own blog. Amazon is becoming a social network of writers. That's a good train to get on — but it's not the only train.

IdieBound, Barnes & Noble Online, Books-A-Million, and many other book retailers accept reader reviews. Social networks such as LibraryThing, LinkedIn, and Goodreads also offer reviewing opportunities. Reviews are welcome on Facebook, Instagram, Pinterest, and even Twitter. Most of these sites have nonexclusive user agreements that allow you to place posts on other sites. You can also convert your written reviews into video or audio reviews. You'll be surprised at how much more impressive your video reviews sound when they're based on a written script.

Reviewing will result in your writing coming to the attention of the people who make the stuff you review. Review books, and you will quickly get enough free books to start a used bookstore. Review music, and you will be inundated with CDs, thumb drives, and free tickets to shows. Review espresso machines, and you'll probably receive a nice new one within a year. Most of the stuff you receive will be junk, and dealing with the pressure to review it can be a drag. I have interviewed several of the Amazon Hall of Fame book reviewers and found that they are machines, posting up to ten reviews a day, all original writing, some while holding full-time jobs. I recommend that you don't get too carried away with the swag and stick to reviewing those few books, recordings, or videos you are most passionate about.

Recipes

I am passionate about food. When I was a teen I had fantasies of becoming a chef. I spent a lot of time by my mother's side at the stove during my formative years, watching her conduct a four-burner range as though it were a string quartet: allegro here, pianissimo there, spices raining down like cadences of sixteenth notes, her spatula a baton. I'm not a very adventurous cook, and the culinary arts were never really my calling. I had ulterior motives for hanging out in the kitchen. The middle child of nine, I learned early on that helping Mom cook meant helping myself to a little preview of the evening sonata.

I learned enough technique from my mom that, combined with recipes I've adopted over the years, I can fuel our family through most of the workweek, and then we can seek out the artistry of professionals on the weekends. We all know that no one's spaghetti sauce tastes as good as Mom's. Well, sorry, Mom, but as far as my daughter Francesca is concerned, no one's sauce will ever compare with her dad's. You can imagine my delight when her future husband, Aaron, asked her to procure a family recipe for their new kitchen. Yes, this was probably a not very subtle attempt to get into the good graces of a future father-in-law. And it worked!

My recipe for spaghetti sauce was the basis for an article in the newsletter *Continuous Improvement*. Bestselling author Malcolm Gladwell's recipe for spaghetti sauce was the basis for his breakout TED Talk on the subject. What can you tell us about your spaghetti sauce that is both literary and unique? In an earlier chapter, I spoke about doing listening exercises as a way to quickly move from your verbal brain to your writing brain by forcing you to convert sound into alphabet. It works for tasting exercises, too. Try coming up with ten other words or phrases for *sweet*, and you will ignite your writing brain like putting a match to a gas stove.

As of today I am eight pages into my recipe for enchiladas — and I've just gotten to the part where you assemble the filling. By now, you recognize that I am not a well man and that your narrator is in need of therapy. It turns out writing leads to the production of the pleasure hormone alphabet-amine, and I have an excessive amount in my system. I can't help myself. I find it hard to approach any writing assignment, even something as simple as a recipe, without making it an enjoyable excursion into the imagination. Please indulge me a little longer. Let me just give you a little taste, a fingerful to whet your appetite:

PHASE 2: THE MEAT

Take the hamburger out of the fridge and smell it. Does it smell okay? If not, it might still be good. Touch it. If it's not slimy, you can probably get away with it. If it smells bad, is slimy, and is discolored, dry, and brittle around the corners and reddish-brown like the color of tanned leather, and you're having company, I wouldn't use it. Put it back in the fridge, cuss, turn off the onions, look at the dog, and say, "Are you lookin' at me?" — just like Robert De Niro in *Taxi Driver*. I love that scene! Whip out your car keys like you've got a pistol up your sleeve and get your backside down to the nearest market and buy some fresh ground beef, you idiot.

If the beef is good enough, start breaking it into the large frying pan. While you are breaking up the last of the beef, and you hear the rising hiss of searing meat, stop and check out the expression on the dog's face. That is priceless! There is no greater love than that between a dog and his or her owner and a pound of ground beef. Stir the beef with the wooden spoon. Bang the spoon on the edge of the pan three times. Stir the onions. Bang the spoon. Stir the beef. Take a big swig off that Corona, hombre — you have earned it!

Now that I've ensured you won't be making any surprise visits to my house around dinnertime, let me ask you to try something. One day, when you're in the mood, or called upon, as I was, by a family member to share a secret family recipe, why don't you *really* put some family secrets into it? So much flavor is lost in the bland recipes that start with a shopping list and end with "serves six," leaving out all the juicy things that happened between the stove and the kitchen table. Many of writer Raymond Carver's best scenes happen at the dinner table, where the conversation is as close as a knife. In her breakout book, *We the Living,* novelist Ayn Rand displays an uncanny ability to communicate the smells of the awful things prepared and consumed after the Communist Revolution in St. Petersburg, Russia.

Don't approach any writing assignment, even something as simple as a recipe, without making it an enjoyable excursion into the imagination.

I want you to please try to create a family recipe that you can be certain will be handed down for generations to come. Here's your chance to make a meal that feeds the spirit as well as the flesh. I can hardly wait to see what you whip up!

CHAPTER 7

THE FOUR-PART PITCH

It has never been easier to get published than it is right now. Thanks to the ongoing desktop publishing revolution, there are myriad outlets to choose from. In addition to the blogging sites mentioned in the previous chapter, there are websites on every imaginable topic that need content. There are still some newsstand magazines that pay freelance writers, and there are numerous literary magazines that do not pay.

Beneath the upper echelon of the newsstand, there remains a healthy movement for printed zines: regional and local zines, music zines, political zines, fanzines, and other microtopic zines. In the professions, there are scholarly journals, trade journals, and all manner of websites looking for writers. Then there are the remaining newspapers: big daily papers, smaller alternative newsweeklies, rural weeklies, entertainment guides, classified advertisers, gazetteers. With these choices, you can get published today almost at will. You just won't get paid.

Your priority should be to identify good outlets for your

work: places you have an affinity with, places where your writing will fit. Some of these may be paying markets; most won't be. When you send your writing in, do what I do — ask for their customary rate and accept whatever it is. Simple. We're talking about cultivating outlets for your work here. If you're looking for advice on how to grow a business with your writing, you have entered the wrong book. This book is about making a life as a writer, not making a living as a writer. There are many excellent books about making money with your writing that mostly involve using your writing to generate multiple streams of income. The writing won't pay, but hopefully the consulting will.

You make money from your writing by becoming a recognized name familiar to editors of either periodicals or books. Your published writing precedes you. Publishers are paying, in part, for your name. If you already have a household name, such as celebrity status in some field, you can get paid to write. In fact, you can get paid not to write; you can tell your story to a ghostwriter, who will write it for you.

If you are not a celebrity and you want to write, and you want to find outlets for your work, you are in the right book! As you publish your work, you'll find that your name becomes recognized, and you will have an easier time finding paying as well as free-prestige outlets for your work.

Once you have found a few outlets you'd like to write for, how do you go about opening a dialogue with them? Of course, you could just attach your writing to an email and send it. If you have tried that method and are tired of being rejected, I have something for you that works much better.

Over the years, I have developed a formula for pitching that is stunningly effective. Getting journalists to review books is an art form, and it is very similar to getting an agent or editor to consider your writing. I wrote more than two hundred news releases a year for many years running. This pitch has been refined through literally millions of impressions. I've shared it with many writers, and they report the same remarkable results. It is an obvious but irresistible pitch, which means it's probably not original. I'm sure it's a refinement of a basic sales letter formula I learned in school or read in a book. I call it my Four-Part Pitch. The four parts are:

1. Stroke
2. Pitch
3. Credentials
4. Action alternatives

Let's look at these one by one.

The Stroke

Stroke. Pay a compliment to the receiver. Make it genuine, if you can.

This is the element that most distinguishes the Four-Part Pitch from other sales letters. When you say something genuine and positive about the work your receiver is doing, she can't help but take notice. An author named Bob Black, whom I had the privilege of editing for a number of years, once wrote, "That voice is sweetest that sings my song."

Flattery puts the reader in the right frame of mind to receive your pitch. But it's more than just flattery.

The stroke shows that you did your homework. It tells an editor that you actually read her publication. It makes it more likely that she will actually read your pitch. Here's an example of a fairly generic stroke: "I'm a subscriber to your publication and I love what you're doing in the Interview section."

Take a look at the email pitches you receive. How many senders begin by talking about themselves, and how many start by talking about you? It is human nature to be drawn in by writing that is about us. Drawing in the editor, showing respect, and demonstrating a knowledge of the publication will get her to paragraph two.

The Pitch

Pitch. State your request as clearly and economically as possible.

You have one paragraph to make the case for the piece or project you are pitching. Here's an example of an article pitch: "I'm writing to see if you would be interested in seeing a profile I've written of Gary Michael Smith, the author of *Publishing for Small Press Runs*."

Come right out and state your request — no long-winded setup. The hard part is getting your pitch across in one paragraph. You have to take out almost all the hype to get it to fit.

Now that you have attracted the editor's attention with your stroke, and quickly stated your request, it's time to sell yourself as the right person to write this piece.

Your Credentials

Credentials. What qualifications do you have to author this piece?

This paragraph should answer the question, "Okay, I like the idea; what makes you the right person to write it?" This is where you mention any previous writing experience or, if you have a lot of experience, where you stick to credits that will appeal to this specific editor for this assignment.

There is a lot more risk in publishing than many writers realize. One risk is that a writer will blow off the deadline. That could leave an editor scrambling. Editors are always wondering whether the writer will deliver the goods. Another risk is that the piece will be terrible. If you can claim to have been published by a recognized outlet, the editor should be willing to extend the benefit of the doubt that you can probably put sentences together. Another risk is that you will be a jerk about any edits made to your piece. Any experience you have writing for a daily, weekly, or monthly demonstrates a maturity about being edited; you are less likely to consider your writing beyond improvement. Other risks are that you'll violate copyright law, you have an exaggerated opinion of what you should be paid, and so on.

All these risks linger in the mind of an editor or agent considering your pitch. The failings of writers become the failings of editors. You ease these fears with your credentials paragraph. Here's an example: "I'm a freelance writer living in New Orleans. I teach at Tulane University. I write profiles of publishers for *The Independent* and other publishing periodicals. My writing has appeared in *Small Press, Northwest Writer,* and *Salon.*"

"That's easy for you to say," you're thinking, "but what if you don't have any credentials?" Everyone has credentials, trust me. It's more a matter of making your credentials relevant than whether or not you have them. It might take some creativity on your part, but you can get through this paragraph even if you have no significant experience as a published writer. Don't lie about your credentials, because that's easy to spot. You only have to tell enough of the truth to get your foot in the door. We all have enough experience to warrant having our submissions considered by an editor.

Here is some phrasing that might help you through the credentials paragraph. If you have ever been paid to write, you are a professional writer. You don't have to be a full-time, paid writer to be a professional writer; you just have to be paid something as a result of your writing abilities. Does your work involve writing of any kind? Reports, analysis, correspondence? Then a portion of your pay is for your ability to communicate well in writing, you are a professional writer, and you are most likely a subject-matter expert in the things you write about. Wow, you sound pretty good to me!

Now it's time to seal the deal. I used to call the fourth paragraph "the close," as in a sales letter, but the best close is not a close at all, it's an "open," as in keeping your options open.

Action Alternatives

Action alternatives. Don't force the editor into a yes or no position. Instead, provide a variety of suggested outcomes between yes and no.

A close is an attempt to force the decision in your favor,

with lines such as "I hope you'll consider this piece" or "I can complete the piece in two weeks." An open tries to turn even a no into a positive outcome by generating other leads. Here's an example: "If you'd like to see the piece, please let me know what format you prefer. If this profile isn't quite on the mark, would you be receptive to other profile ideas? If you're not in the market for work like this, can you recommend someone who might be? I appreciate your consideration and look forward to hearing from you."

In those few cases where I have not been given the green light to submit a piece for consideration, I get suggestions for other stories the editor would like to see. Sometimes I get referrals to editors at other publications. Then I have a built-in stroke for the next query letter: "I was referred to you by Jane Smith, the editor of…"

What's Missing?

Let's take a look at what we left out in order to create such an economical query letter.

- **Money.** Never mention compensation in a pitch letter. There's plenty of time for that later. I usually ask for whatever the publication's customary and standard rate of pay is, and I accept that the first time. Maybe after a few pieces get published and I have established a relationship, I'll see if there is room to negotiate a higher fee.
- **Rights.** There should be no mention of "first serial rights" or any other language related to copyright or

usage restrictions. It's premature to mention rights in a pitch letter. When I submit a piece, I usually state the rights arrangement I want at the top and let the publisher ask for something different if they need it. I usually begin a piece with "First Serial Rights to *Publication Name*." When the editors want exclusive rights, they usually aren't bashful about asking for them.

- **Ultimatums.** You want to avoid hostile-sounding language such as, "If I haven't heard from you in two weeks, I'll assume I'm at liberty to pitch this idea elsewhere." You don't play hardball in a pitch letter; you play softball — a nice, gentle pitch that's easy to hit and makes the batter look good.

- **The piece itself.** Do not include the piece with your pitch. There are exceptions to the rule, but this is a common pitching mistake made by beginning writers. They're so anxious for someone to see what they've written that they can't restrain themselves from including it with the pitch letter. By sending a pitch only, you're following protocol and showing respect for your editor's time.

The Mysterious Maggie Thrash

The Four-Part Pitch works so well I can hardly believe it. It's been the basis for hundreds of pitches I've written myself. Numerous students have used it to find jobs. It just never occurs to many writers that they should spend some time getting to know the person on the other end of the pitch *before* launching it. There is no more beautiful example of how this pitch can transform even a first-time writer into a published author with a major contract than Maggie Thrash. Her first email arrived on December 8, 2010.

"Hi, it's Maggie Thrash, Laura's bridesmaid. I was in attendance at Uncle Steve's Post-Wedding Bash last year, if you recall. I am a novelist (YA), and am thinking about self-publishing (sick of rejection letters, want to be empowered!)."

I responded, "Self-publishing is a pain and you should do everything you can to avoid it. I have a fairly foolproof method for landing an agent and/or an editor. It's worth the effort and time."

Together, we composed a pitch letter. The stroke was easy. Maggie was in thrall with the book *Girl* by Blake Nelson, whose agent is literary legend Judith Regan. The book was serialized in *Sassy* magazine under editor Christina Kelly before Nelson secured Regan as his agent. We made a list of several other books Maggie admired or aspired to, then we found the agents for those authors using Amazon's "Search Inside This Book" feature and searching for "agent." Here's the opening of her Four-Part Pitch: "You have a medal in my book as the person who spotted *Girl* and brought it to life. I'm hoping you will be interested in another author who, like Blake Nelson, is a nobody with a great YA voice."

It's the credentials paragraph where we hit a wall. Maggie Thrash had no writing credits. None. After some significant wordsmithing, we came up with this: "I am currently working with Chris Bachelder of *McSweeneys* and *Bear v. Shark* at the Sewanee School of Letters, where I will receive a master's in English and creative writing. I offer grammar and editing workshops to library science students at UNC Chapel Hill and have appeared in the *Raleigh News and Observer*."

Here's the condensed version of what happened after this pitch went out.

- **January 2011:** Maggie sends her pitch to Christina Kelly, who asks to see the sample chapter and forwards it to Shana Corey, an editor at Random House.
- **February 2011:** I encourage Maggie Thrash to get an agent. "If Shana Corey is looking at your work, any agent would be happy to have you."
- **May 2012:** More than a year later, Maggie writes, "I continue to apply your principles of flattery and persistence." Two top literary agents want to represent her. One of them is interested in having her do a graphic novel based on some comics she has online. She signs with Stephen Barr at Writers House, a top literary agency.
- **September 2015:** *Honor Girl*, a graphic novel by Maggie Thrash, is published by Candlewick Press to critical acclaim.
- **October 2016:** *We Know It Was You*, a YA murder mystery by Maggie Thrash, is published by Simon & Schuster Pulse.
- **August 2017:** *We Know It Was You* is repackaged as *Strange Truth* and published with Maggie Thrash's next book, *Strange Lies*.

If Maggie Thrash, a college student with no writing credits, can get one of the world's top literary agents at Writers House and then get published by Simon & Schuster on the basis of a killer query letter and the writing chops to back it up, then certainly you can do the same. Why don't you outline your pitch letter right now and send it off as soon as possible?

WRITING EXERCISE

THE FOUR-PART PITCH

Your assignment is to write a four-paragraph pitch for one of the publications you would like to write for. Only four paragraphs — how hard is that? It shouldn't take longer than twenty minutes to complete this exercise.

1. **Stroke.** Pay a compliment to the receiver of the query letter. Make it genuine, if you can.
2. **Pitch.** State your request as clearly and economically as possible.
3. **Credentials.** What qualifications do you have to author this piece?
4. **Action alternatives.** Don't force the editor into a yes or no position. Instead, provide a variety of suggested outcomes between yes and no.

If you use this pitch, you will likely get published or get a referral. If you follow up on those referrals, research the contacts, and write convincing strokes, you should be able to keep enough work in production to feel like you are making some real progress on a writing career.

CHAPTER 8

SEEKING COMMERCIAL PUBLICATION

Having a book published is the ultimate goal of most writers and even many nonwriters. The desire to see one's name on the binding of a book on a library or store shelf can be overwhelming. It is so intoxicating that thousands of people are willing to devote thousands of dollars and thousands of hours to making that vision real, without any consideration for financial return.

Do You Want to Be an Author or a Publisher?

If you want to be a writer, you should write. If you want to be a published writer, you should work very hard to find other people to publish your work. You should not try to publish your work yourself unless you want to be an entrepreneur, accepting all the responsibilities and privileges thereof.

I work with a dozen authors every year who are somewhere in the matrix among manuscript, self-publishing, and commercial publishing. The unhappiest of this group are those who have self-published and are unable to find buyers or reviewers for their books. The most frustrated are those with manuscripts who are seeking publishers and contemplating investing their own money for a reasonable print run. The least unhappy are the commercially published authors. I can't call them "happy" because so many of them are upset at how their publishers brought their books into print and how little their publishers are doing to promote their books. No one in publishing is happy except UPS; they get paid to move hot sellers to market, and they get paid to move the losers to the recycling bin. Everyone else — writers, agents, editors, designers, publishers, printers, sales reps, distributors, wholesalers, publicists, reviewers, store clerks — is more or less struggling daily to survive.

When you are trying to win over an agent or editor, this struggle is the conversation you are walking into. It can be discouraging, intimidating, and brutal. You can easily get worn down after only five rejections and shelve your plans for publication permanently. Still, after many years of having shared the lives of people on all stages of this path, I'd say it's worth spending months or even years of your life trying to find a commercial publisher for your work rather than embarking on the expensive, risky path of self-publishing. Unless you are intentionally publishing a limited print run for your family and friends, you are going to be happier as a published writer than you are as a publisher. Let me spend a little time showing you some devastatingly effective ways of interesting an agent and an editor in your work.

Pitch Letter Freak Show

The secret to getting a book published by a commercial house is to find people, not publishers. Publishing companies don't respond to proposals — people do. There are two people, at most, that stand between you and publication: an *acquisitions editor* and a *literary agent*. Your job is to find out who those two people are — their names, their backgrounds, their contact information — and then pitch to them. Think of the pitching process as an act of seduction, and you're well on your way to publication.

Ah, the art of seduction. It's more about listening than talking, isn't it? It's about little gestures that send signals. It's about encouraging the response you want without directly asking for it. It's about smoothing the path for a positive reply rather than forcing the other with threats or ultimatums. The seduction is a tease, and the first part of the tease is the introduction: the pitch letter.

Here is the first paragraph of a query letter given to me by my boss, Mike Hoy, when I worked as editorial director at Loompanics Unlimited. See if you can spot anything wrong with this writer's approach.

Attention Editor in Chief
Michael Hoy

Dear Mr. Hoy
I have wrote a manuscrip and seeking favorable marketing of same. It is composed of 254 type-written

pages. The basic contents of the manuscrip concerns the legal profession in America, a southern legal law firm' practices and functions, horse racing, the civil war ers... Lincoln, the struggle of union labor movement in America, the early settlors city of Seattle and quite a few of my own personal exploitations during the course of my life as a lawyer, laborer and reconnaissancer of good and bad people. The entire book is predicated upon truths with fiction, glamour and humor added to flavour the ultimate.

Wow, that's original! I have carried around this query letter for decades as though it were some aboriginal masterpiece — outsider word work at its finest. Now whenever you think your attempts to find a publisher are hopeless, repeat after me: "I have wrote a manuscrip." That is what you're up against. Surely you can do better. Surely there is room for you in the pantheon of published writers.

I didn't ask to see this gentleman's manuscrip, but actually his pitch is not as horrible as it may at first sound. Yes, he has trouble with grammar, but so what — as long as he can tell a good story. The jump from a southern law firm and the Civil War to Seattle gave me geographical whiplash. Still, the author took the time to find the name of someone at Loompanics to send his pitch to. More than 95 percent of the pitches we received at Loompanics did not begin with anyone's name. This pitch letter does include several topic categories Loompanics published: law, work, gambling, corruption. He might have a good yarn or two in him — possibly enough to make it worth cleaning up the grammar. But I didn't ask to see his manuscrip.

Let's take a look at one more opening paragraph from a pitch letter I received recently via email.

To: Steve O'Keefe

Subject: MY BOOK

HELLO, I HAVE A SMALL 8 1/2 BY 11 INCH BOOK OF POEMS. IT IS A MOTIVATIONAL AND SPIRITUAL BOOK WITH 74 PAGES, WRITTEN IN CHRONOLOGICAL ORDER. ABOUT THE MANY HAPPENINGS OF MY DAILY LIFE EXPERIENCES.

Whoa, that is special! Do you see a common thread here? Both opening paragraphs state the size of the book within the first two sentences. It's as though your best pitch is girth and that publishers purchase books based on length. I think it's just nervousness, a novice writing about something personal to someone unknown. How do you begin? Most writers begin by describing the book. These writers describe it physically: its length and trim size. This is classic writer's warm-up; as you know, the first few paragraphs of most sessions at the keyboard can safely be discarded.

I admire that the writer of this last pitch letter is attempting to better understand his life by writing about it. He has gotten up the nerve to share his writing with others and try to get it published. His pitching technique, however, could use a little work. Surely, you can do better. So why don't you try, right now, to write the opening sentences of a pitch letter for a book you'd like to write.

WRITING EXERCISE
THE STROKE

Write the first part of your Four-Part Pitch, the stroke. Write one or two sentences, and don't mention anything about your book or about you. Explain why you have chosen the person on the receiving end of your pitch.

Finding Editors and Agents

Do you find it hard to write two sentences about someone you don't know? I do. So how do you find the name of the person to address your query letter to? At large publishing companies, you look for an acquisitions editor. At smaller houses, you might target an editor, editorial director, or publisher/owner. At a literary agency, you look for the names of individual agents. People act as if it's impossible to locate the names of these professionals. It's not. It's easy.

Jeff Herman's Guide to Book Publishers, Editors & Literary Agents is the only reference work you need. Revised annually, it is currently in its twenty-eighth edition. Where other books give you contact information for publishing companies and literary agencies, Herman's book gives you the names and job titles of individual agents and acquisitions editors. This info is priceless for pitching. You can and should contact the publishing company in advance of mailing your pitch to verify the spelling of the contact person's name, thus finding out if he or she still works there. You can also find lists of editors and agents online. The two best online lists I've found are AgentQuery.com, a free database of literary agents; and Publishers Marketplace (by subscription at www.publishers marketplace.com). But there's another good way to find the names of these people, thanks to Amazon.com.

Amazon offers a free service called "Search Inside This Book," available for many of the most popular books in the company's giant database. Type in a keyword, such as *editor* or *agent*, and the search engine reveals every occurrence of that word in the book. Pick an author you admire, or a bestselling book in the category you hope to publish in, and search for "agent" and "editor." Nine times out of ten, the author will thank his or her agent or editor somewhere in the book. The names of those editors and agents will appear in Amazon's search results. This same service can often be accessed through Google Books, IndieBound, Barnes & Noble, and other large book databases. You might have to check several of them to find an agent's or editor's name.

If you write crime fiction, you can use Amazon.com to find the top crime fiction agents and editors in the country — people who work with such authors as *A Is for Alibi* author Sue Grafton. If you write children's books, you'll be surprised how easy it is to find agents and editors who handle authors such as J. K. Rowling or Mary Pope Osborne or Philip Pullman. With just an hour or two of playing around on Amazon, you should be able to find the names of two or three agents and four or five editors. You'll also know something about them: the names of writers these editors and agents have handled in the past, and some of the book titles they've helped bring into print.

If you want, you can learn a little more about these editors and agents by googling them. Type their exact names into the Google search bar and see what pops up. Publishing is a profession populated by wordsmiths. With top agents and editors, a Google search will often bring up something they've written. Maybe they've authored books themselves, or articles about the craft, or short stories, or poems. Knowing that will help you with your stroke paragraph. Sometimes you'll find interviews with agents and editors, and those usually contain precious insights that can be used in a pitch.

I taught a class in writing book proposals at the Erma Bombeck Humor Writers' Workshop at the University of Dayton in Ohio. Attendees were mostly humor writers looking for inspiration and outlets for their work. We pulled up the book page at Amazon.com for a book by humorist Dave Barry, then searched the book for "agent." There were five instances of "agent" in this book. The first four were to law enforcement agents. Here's match number five:

> from the front matter:
> …character that she has never, to my knowledge, turned to heroin. Finally, I thank my editor, Sam Vaughan, and my **agent**, Al Hart, without whom I might have to get a real job.

Bingo! I'd like to thank my author, Dave Barry, and my search engine, Amazon.com, without whom I might have spent several hours finding the names of this editor and agent.

In the Bombeck writers' workshop, we went to Google and searched for "Sam Vaughan" and "Al Hart" and found mailing addresses, phone numbers, and email addresses for both of them within two screen jumps. "Al Hart" turns out to be A. L. Hart, with the Fox Chase Agency in King of Prussia, Pennsylvania. We found an interview with Random House editor Sam Vaughan dating from 1999. The author of the interview met with Vaughan three times in person, and also interviewed authors Vaughan had mentored. Does that interview contain insights that can be used in the stroke paragraph of a pitch letter addressed to Sam Vaughan? You bet it does!

Try this exercise yourself. Make a mental or written note to find a couple of editors and agents next time you're at Amazon.com. Then write down their names and contact information:

Contact Information for My Soon-to-Be Agent:

Contact Information for My Soon-to-Be Editor:

Can You Pitch by Email?

Of course you can. You can pitch any way you want. If you learn that it's against "company policy" to accept pitches via email, don't worry about it. You're not communicating with a company — you're communicating with a person. Even when an editor or agent does say, "I don't like to be pitched by email," they most likely mean, "Please don't pitch anything I'm not interested in, regardless of the method you use to pitch."

Here's an interesting observation about pitching to editors via email, from the opening paragraph of an article by the *Wall Street Journal*'s longtime publishing industry reporter, Jeffrey Trachtenberg:

> Like many publishing houses, Walt Disney Co.'s Hyperion has a policy against reading unsolicited manuscripts or book queries. But last December, Editor-in-Chief Will Schwalbe opened an e-mail message with "Fireman's wife" in the subject line, thinking it concerned the David Halberstam book he had edited. Instead, it was a brief pitch that read, in part, "I am coping. Often I am lonely, I am surprised, I am underpaid. But in a relationship that defines my identity, I am the fireman's wife." Mr. Schwalbe was hooked.

Let's check that pitch a little more closely. The grammar is not the Queen's English. These could be the opening lines of a homemaker's memoirs — a pitch agents and editors see every day but that seldom brings a response. Why did this author get a response? Why did Mr. Schwalbe immediately reach for the phone and call the author of that pitch? Why were her "memoirs of a fireman's wife" deemed worthy to be published by a major commercial house when so many others have been rejected?

Susan Farren, the author of this pitch, didn't write to

Hyperion. Hyperion has a policy against reading anything unsolicited. She pitched to Will Schwalbe, whose policy on unsolicited email is a little more liberal. I'll bet you the advance on your next book that Susan Farren knew that Schwalbe had edited Halberstam's book, that she found Schwalbe's name in the acknowledgments in one of Halberstam's books, and that she did a little research or guesswork to arrive at Mr. Schwalbe's primary email address. Her subject line is itself a stroke, quickly communicating "I know who you are and something of what you've done. It is no accident you are getting this email. This is probably not spam." All that information is communicated between Farren and Schwalbe with two simple words — *Fireman's wife* — in the subject line.

A friend of mine, Susan Solakian, had "wrote a manuscrip" and was seeking favorable marketing of same. Her pitches to fourteen literary agents brought thirteen rejections and one nondeliverable. We went through the Amazon/Google research process together, identified four top agents, researched their backgrounds, and pitched them all via email. The same day we pitched, we received three personal responses: two polite rejections and a request for the book proposal from superstar literary agent Bob Diforio. Solakian used a standard Four-Part Pitch as the cover letter for the book proposal. The opening lines were:

> Your agency has closed so many great deals with major publishers for books like mine that I'm happy to enclose, at your request, the book proposal for *A Homeowner's Guide to Managing a Renovation.*

Within twenty-four hours, Mr. Diforio responded:

Dear Susan,
This is really impressive.
I am sure I will want to represent you and the book.
Here is our standard author's agreement.
Let me know if you have any questions.
Best,
Bob

Susan had spent two agonizing years shopping that manuscript, looking for an agent or a publisher. In two short days
after learning about the Four-Part Pitch, she landed on the
roster of a top literary agency. With the right pitch to the
right person, you can find representation just as quickly.

Listening to the Bookstore

When pitching to a literary agent or book publisher, you
should begin with a trip to the bookstore and ask yourself,
"Where will my book be shelved?" Go to that spot and stop.
Take a good look at the author to your left and to your right.
Bookstore shelves are usually organized by genre or topic,
then alphabetized by author last name. It should be easy to
spot who your shelf mates will be. Pick up copies of your new
neighbors, browse their back covers, tables of contents, and
copyright pages. Who publishes them? Take notes.

Now look for the category killers. Which books are displayed face out? Which books are stocked in numbers greater
than three copies per title? Who are the kings and queens of

the shelves? How did they get there? Open their books, write down the names of their publishers. See if they thank their editors and agents in the acknowledgments. You will leave the bookstore with a small family of authors (well, names of authors) who rule your section of the bookstore. You need to be able to explain how you can sell in the shadows they cast.

You can perform this by listening online as well, but it doesn't substitute for a trip to the bookstore. You need to see the physical attributes of these books — the illustrations, the paper stock, the bindings, the trim size. Listening online will give you another perspective. Who rules your turf at Amazon.com? What are the bestsellers in your category? What books in your category are most like yours? How do their sales ranks compare with the category killers? Who published these books, who edited them, who agented them?

You should be able to find the names of five publishing companies that are prime targets for your pitch. Visit their websites. What categories does this publisher sustain? Which books are featured, and why? How do they talk about the books in their catalogs? Is the writing style effervescent? professional? snooty? deep? Many publishers include marketing information on their websites, such as the size of a book's print run, the publication date, and author tour cities.

What page of the website will your book be on? What will they say about your book? Imagine the print run they will allocate to your title and the marketing budget they will provide for it. Can you see yourself on that website? If yes, write your page. If no, you may need to change your approach to the book or look for a publisher that offers a better fit.

This fantasy — seeing yourself in the bookstore, seeing

yourself on Amazon, seeing yourself on a publisher's website — can cripple your writing, causing you to veer away from what is in your heart to what will sell. Once your writing smells like something written to sell, agents and editors lose their appetite. What should matter to you when you write is that you get it right — that it comes across on the page the way it feels inside, that you set the page on fire. Focusing on making your book popular is something you can worry about later. Somehow, you have to get through this exercise without losing your passion for the project. It's not easy.

Here is my recommendation: Always remember that you are talented, original, and have something important to say. Listen to yourself most of all. Write down what you hear.

Are You Ready for Yes?

Tim Bete, the humor columnist who was codirector of the Erma Bombeck Humor Writers' Workshop, asked for my advice on finding an agent for a collection of his humorous stories about parenting. I showed him the Four-Part Pitch and the Amazon/Google research routine, and he expressed disbelief that he should not include the proposal or a writing sample with his query. I explained that he needed to have the proposal prepared and ready to go upon request but should never include it with the pitch email. Make them ask to see it.

Tim sent out the pitch, but he wasn't ready for "yes." He didn't have his book proposal ready to go. I'll let Tim pick up the story. This is from his diary, *Anatomy of a First Book*:

I didn't find an agent but received some useful feedback through the rejections. I learned how to create a better proposal and book concept.

Because several agents wanted to see a complete proposal and sample chapters, I was forced to create the proposal I should have created in the first place....

I pitched six or seven Christian publishers. Three publishers requested a proposal and sample chapters. Two [of these] offered contracts.

Wow. Seven pitches. Three publishers asked for the book proposal. Two offered contracts. Trust me, it's not easy to sell a collection of humorous essays on parenting. Almost all parents have enough funny stories to fill a book. Very few get to write such a book, fewer still get one published.

You need to be ready for "yes" when you pitch. You need to be prepared for the many positive responses you'll receive when you follow the advice in this book.

When Is It Over?

In 2004 I went to Port Townsend, Washington, to write a book about writing, and what I found was Professor Emeritus T. A. Guillory. To look at him, you would not think he was approaching the end of his life but that he had already passed it. He was gaunt and walked stooped over, dressed in worn-out clothes that were tattered but clean. The windows of his car were tinted on the inside with a thick, tacky coating of cigarette smoke residue. The seats in his car were piled high with newspapers, mail, and manuscript pages. He was wealthy from mineral rights he owned back in Louisiana, but he lived like a pauper in a trailer at the edge of town. He wanted to surprise his son with all the money he had saved.

Professor Guillory was the local curmudgeon in the *Port Townsend Leader.* That was how he kept his muse close. The author of several books, he also taught a writers' workshop in a historic building downtown. He had taught English at Washington, Idaho, and Purdue Universities. Imagine his surprise upon going into the classroom for perhaps the last time in 2004 and finding a wordslinger from Cajun Country come up to call him out. The blood came up in his face like an amaryllis on New Year's Day.

During the class session on writer's block, Guillory kept repeating, "The hard part is not getting started. It's knowing when to stop." A wry smile twisted his face as he waited for a response. "How do you know when it's finished?" he asked.

"When you put a stamp on it and put it in the mail," I replied. He referred to me as an intelligent mule — or words to that effect — but I was serious. That's how you know when it's done: when you send it to someone. That's what it means to be published (literally, "to make public"). It's that simple. Write down what you hear, put a stamp on it, send it to someone. Send it to me, if you want, but just get rid of it. Then keep going. Once you set the page on fire, it's hard to put it out.

How *do* you put it out? I take a shower. That usually knocks down the burn enough so I can go to work. How do you know when it's finished? You put a stamp on it and send it off in the mail (or you email it). You publish it. It's that simple.

If you have made your way through this book and you have not sent me something you've written, I have failed. If you do send me something, and I hope you will, you will most likely get back a polite "thank you." What else is there to say? That's what any good mentor will tell you. Make your alphabet and mail it. The rest is a distraction.

How do you know when it's over? The truth is, it never ends. I can still hear Professor Guillory's magnolia voice. I can still hear Brenda Ueland: "Tell me more!" I can't, however, hear you. Speak up. I'm listening.

ACKNOWLEDGMENTS

Publishing Professionals Interviewed for
Set the Page on Fire

Judith Appelbaum (1940–2018), author of *How to Get Happily Published*

Dan Poynter (1938–2015), publisher, author of *Dan Poynter's Self-Publishing Manual*

Melvin Charles Jones, Sr. (1931–2014), proprietor, A Tisket A Tasket Booksellers

Peter Workman (1938–2013), publisher, Workman Publishing

Phil Wood (1938–2010), publisher, Ten Speed Press

Jan Nathan (1939–2007), executive director, Publishers Marketing Association

T. A. Guillory, professor emeritus of English, University of Washington and Purdue

John Huenefeld, consultant, author of *The Huenefeld Guide to Book Publishing*

Michael Hoy, publisher, Loompanics Unlimited. He taught me book publishing.

Alice B. Acheson, celebrated book publicist and my mentor

Jeff Herman, literary agent, author of *Jeff Herman's Guide to Book Publishers, Editors & Literary Agents,* and my agent

Gary Michael Smith, publisher, author of *Publishing for Small Press Runs*

Rick Wilks, director, Annick Press

Pam Art, publisher, Storey Publishing

Dominique Raccah, publisher, Sourcebooks

Maggie Lichtenberg, book publishing coach

John Kremer, author of *1001 Ways to Market Your Books*

Ken McCarthy, publisher, author of *System Secrets*

Marcella Smith, former director of Small Press and Vendor Relations,
Barnes & Noble

Richard Hoy, cofounder, BookLocker.com

Jeff Bezos, founder, Amazon.com

Authors and Others Interviewed for
Set the Page on Fire

Franklin Adams	Rene Broussard	Jocelyn Elder
Jennifer Adams	Juanita Brown	Jill Ellsworth
Carol Adrienne	Betsy Burton	Chris Epting
Joel Agee	Rev. Goat Carson	Janet Eyring
Dorothy Allison	Betsy Carter	Robert Fanney
Amanda Anderson	Paula Chase-Hyman	Patricia Hale Feeney
Christophe Andersson	Ethan Clark	Virginna Fleck
Rexanne Becnel	Joshua Clark	Glenn Fleishman
Tom Benjey	Andrei Codrescu	Dennis Foon
Jason Berry	Andrew Connan	Ken Foster
Tim Bete	Joe Cook	Peter Francis
Michael C. Bevis	Debra Cox	Tripp Friedler
John Billheimer	Antonio Crawford	GiO
B. D. Blanchard	Louie Crowder	Peter Gloor
Renee Bobb	Carla Danziger	Scott Gold
Steven Boone	g. k. darby	Neil Gordon
Edward J. Branley	Pamela Davis-Noland	Shari Graydon
Kyle Bravo	R. C. Deglinkta	Jonathan Gross
Susannah Breslin	Michael "Rex" Dingler	Lee Meitzen Grue
Jay Brida	Robin Donovan	T. A. Guillory
Poppy Z. Brite	Don Dunnington	Amy Guth

Haley Haden
Stephen Harrigan
Richard Harris
Susan Harrow
Pat Hartman
Patricia Heller
Ina Hillebrandt
Abram Himelstein
Sarah Honenberger
Ruth Hoppin
Shel Horowitz
Mike Hoy
Richard Hoy
Daniel Hoyer
Will Hutchison
Sandra Ingerman
George Ingmire
Sarah Inman
David Isaacs
Shelley Lynn Jackson
Molly Bruce Jacobs
Reginald Johns
Dedra Johnson
Gavin S. Johnson
Frank S. Joseph
Eric Julien
Chef Katrina
Romy Kaye
N. M. Kelby
David Koen
Paul Krupin
Vicki Lane
Jon Lebkowsky
Loris Lesynski
Maggie Lichtenberg

Kathryn Lively
Joan Logghe
Suzanne Lopez
Pat MacEnulty
Mike Maranhas
Michael Martchenko
Chris Matherne
Jacqueline May
Ken McCarthy
Caesar Meadows
Keith Welden Medley
William C. Miller
Ann Conti Morcos
Robert Munsch
Christopher David
    Murphy
Coleen Murphy
Jessica Nagler
Laryssa Nechay
Nick Nechay
Carly Newfeld
James Newton
Bob O'Connor
Ruth Ohi
Chris Ortiz
Oz
Chuck Panozzo
Josh Peter
Janet Peterson
Valentine Pierce
Elaine Pinkerton
Dr. Milo Pinkerton III
Emily Pohl-Weary
John Pritchard
Linda Rainwater

Barbara Rath, MD
Chris Reese
Rob Reider
Robert Rhine
Rev. R. Tony Ricard
Robb Roemershauser
Jacob Rosenberg
Marilyn Ross
Linda Salisbury
Margaret Sartor
Doc Saxtrum
Ned Schumann
Ellen Augustine
    Schwartz
Angelle Scott
David Meerman Scott
Jerry Sears
Louise Shaffer
Maggie Oman
    Shannon
Sharon Short
Jennie Shortridge
Ningay Sing
Rebecca Skeele
Robert Smallwood
Gary Michael Smith
Susan Solakian
Joan Sotkin
Karen Southwick
Allan Stratton
Diane Swanson
Xavier T.
Jose Torres Tama
Robert Tannen
Mike Tanner

Joe Taylor
R. Scott Taylor
Gary Thomas
Verita Thompson
Maggie Thrash
James Tormey
TVS and Two Fingers
Elizabeth Underwood
Rita Valley

Tim Van Schmidt
Lance Vargas
Vanessa Vega
Johanna Vondeling
Tedd M. Walley
Maureen Walsh
Eric Ward
Martha Ward
Heather Weathers

Steve Weber
Michael Welch
David S. White
Rick Wilks
Jenny Williams
Steve Williams
Alice Wilson-Fried
Dr. Stanley Wolf
Lawrence Wright

Colleagues Who Helped *Set the Page on Fire*

Marc Allen
Antero Alli
Kate Bandos
Marianna Barry
Don Bates
Suzanne Bosse
Holly Brady
Connie Brand
Bob Burjoice
Robin Caputo
Sarah Chayes
Linda Civello
Peter Clifton
Kim Corbin
Jocelyn Cordova
James A. Cox
Elijah Cross
Cate Cummings
Mark Dazzo
Jacqueline Deval
John Deveney
Susan Diaz-Romero

Ellie Dodson
Eileen Duhne
Jason Epstein
Coley Evans
Cynthia Frank
Mark Frauenfelder
Gwendolyn Gawlick
Ellen Reavis Gerstein
Lynn Goldberg
Norm Goldman
Patrick Grace
Paul Greenberg
Susannah Greenberg
Tracey Greene
Jeremy Hart
Georgia Hughes
Kelly Hughes
George Ingmire
T. R. Johnson
Hank Jones
Heidi Krupp
Cliff Kurtzman

Mimi Kusch
Leanne Landers
Tonya Lehner
Chris Lenois
Steve LeVine
Munro Magruder
Irene Majuk
Rachelle Matherne
Carmela Mayson
Kennedy Mbuvi
Ken McCarthy
Katie McCaskey
Vanessa McGrady
John McHugh
Tatyana
    Meshcheryakova
Lori Sayde Mehrtens
Maureen Moss
Walt Mossberg
Monique
    Muhlenkamp
Raj Mukhopadhyay

Terry Nathan
B. L. Ochman
Tom Person
Amy Philips
Dr. Robert Pretlow
Lyndsey Rabon
Keith Reeves
Rachel Reeves
David Reich
Howard Rheingold
Andrea Millen Rich
Chug Roberts
Anthony Roland
M. J. Rose
Lew Routh
Heath Row
Morty Schiller

Betsy Scuteri
Katherine Shute
Sandy Siegle
Gibbs Smith
Patricia Spadaro
Joan Stewart
Heather Stone
Victoria Sutherland
Mohammed
    Tazehzadeh
Laura Theriot
Kama Timbrell
Richard R. Troxell
Rob Van Slyke
Lance Vargas
Jesse Vohs
Carol Vorvian

Melissa Weiner
Kelley Weir
Kim Weiss
Allyson Wendt
Skye Wentworth
Creamy Whitethighs
Kathleen Jacob
    Wikstrom
David Wilk
George "Loki"
    Williams
Hilary Williamson
Scott Wilson
Tom Woll
Nigel Yorwerth
Marcia Yudkin
Alex Zorychta

Organizations That Assisted with *Set the Page on Fire*

The Stanford Professional Publishing Program
The Independent Book Publishers Association (IBPA),
    formerly Publishers Marketing Association (PMA)
The Community of Literary Magazines and Presses (CLMP)
The Association for the Export of Canadian Books (AECB)
The Ontario Book Publishers Association (OBPO)
The Book Publishers Association of Alberta (BPAA)
Publishers Association of the West (PubWest)
The Public Relations Society of America (PRSA)
The American Society of Association Executives (ASAE)
The Erma Bombeck Humor Writers' Workshop

Family and Friends Who Helped *Set the Page on Fire*

Brian T. O'Keefe
(1925–2003)
RoseAnn O'Keefe
Tom O'Keefe
Mike O'Keefe
Diane O'Keefe
Maureen O'Keefe
Cousins
Kelly O'Keefe
Cristy Drake O'Keefe
Barry O'Keefe

Sharon O'Keefe
Newlon
Janet O'Keefe
Storme O'Keefe
Francesca O'Keefe
Wolf
Aaron Deter-Wolf
Deborah O'Keeffe
Chelsea Vance
Tom McClanaghan
Kathleen O'Keefe
McClanaghan

Leslie Graves Key
O'Keefe
Eric O'Keefe
Seraphim O'Keefe
Thomas E. O'Keefe
Barry Wilder O'Keefe
Donald S. O'Keefe
Stephen Boyer Wallace
Gerald Wayne
Strickland
James Scranton

NOTES

Chapter 2. You Can Do This!

p. 23　*Brenda Ueland, author of* If You Want to Write: Brenda Ueland, *If You Want to Write: A Book about Art, Independence, and Spirit* (Middletown, RI: BN Publishing, 2010). This phrase comes from the title of chapter 1.

p. 35　*I once interviewed the world's most famous*: John Huenefeld, *The Huenefeld Guide to Book Publishing,* 3rd ed. (Bedford, MA: Huenefeld Co., 1986); interview available at http://articles.ibpa -online.org/article/john-huenefeld-helping-mid-sized-firms -prosper.

Chapter 3. Listening for Good Writing

p. 42　*Who Killed My Dog Robert*: *Port Townsend Leader,* letter to the editor, July 1990.

p. 44　*The writer has a feeling and utters it*: Brenda Ueland, *If You Want to Write: A Book about Art, Independence, and Spirit,* "Preface to the Second Edition" (St. Paul, MN: Graywolf Press, 1987), xi.

p. 48　*What is the source of the atrocious sentence*: *Writing on the Edge* 5, no. 1 (1993), 14.

p. 50   *Get out truthfully what is in you*: Brenda Ueland, *If You Want to Write: A Book about Art, Independence, and Spirit* (Middletown, RI: BN Publishing, 2010), 52.

p. 51   *And here's a nice passage from a book*: Mark Roskill, ed., *The Letters of Vincent van Gogh* (New York: Penguin, 1996), letter to Theo, March 1882.

p. 51   *The best comedy is informed*: Trevor Noah, interview by Chuck Todd, MSNBC, October 31, 2018, https://www.msnbc.com/mtp -daily/watch/trevor-noah-on-what-it-means-to-be-political -in-the-trump-era-1358473283532.

Chapter 4. Thinking, Talking, Writing, Reading

p. 60   *A study of the meaning of spoken words*: Philip Yaffe, "The 7% Rule: Fact, Fiction, or Misunderstanding," *Ubiquity* (October 2011): 1–5, https://ubiquity.acm.org/article.cfm?id=2043156.

p. 62   *It is a mistake for a sculptor*: Henry Moore, "Notes on Sculpture," in *The Creative Process: Reflections on the Invention in the Arts and Sciences*, ed. Brewster Ghiselin (Berkeley and Los Angeles, University of California Press, 1985), 68.

p. 64   *Art should be a process of discovery*: Jim Harrison, in Sybil Steinberg, ed., *Writing for Your Life: Ninety-Two Contemporary Authors Talk about the Art of Writing and the Job of Publishing* (New York: Pushcart Press, 1992).

Chapter 5. Making Time to Write

p. 73   *When I wrote* Publicity on the Internet: Steve O'Keefe, *Publicity on the Internet: Creating Successful Publicity Campaigns on the Internet and the Commercial Online Services* (New York: Wiley, 1997).

p. 75   *Getting started is hard*: Ursula K. Le Guin, *Conversations on Writing* (Portland, OR: Tin House, 2018), 95.

p. 75   *The secret of being interesting*: Brenda Ueland, *If You Want to*

Write: A Book about Art, Independence, and Spirit (Middletown, RI: BN Publishing, 2010), 113.

p. 76　*There is so much to love*: Mary Lou Sanelli, *Port Townsend Leader*, July 2004.

Chapter 6. Easy Outlets for Your Writing

p. 97　*Dr. Tel Franklin wrote a book*: Tel Franklin, MD, *Expect a Miracle: You Won't Be Disappointed* (Santa Ana, CA: Center for Appreciative Dialogue, 2003).

Chapter 8. Seeking Commercial Publication

p. 136　*Like many publishing houses, Walt Disney*: Jeffrey Trachtenberg, *Wall Street Journal*, July 1, 2004, https://authorlink.com/news /publishers-warming-to-e-mail-queries-wsj-article-says-2.

p. 141　*I didn't find an agent*: Tim Bete, *Anatomy of a First Book* (University of Dayton, Erma Bombeck Writers' Workshop, August 2004), http://archive.li/qimDG#selection-1308.1-1344.0.

ABOUT THE AUTHOR

S teve O'Keefe is an author, editor, and book-industry professional who has helped hundreds of writers move from brainstorm to bestseller! He has worked with prison writers, Pulitzer Prize winners, college students, and students in adult writing programs. As the content director for Oroborα, Inc., he has hired dozens of expert writers and editors to produce a steady stream of articles, blog posts, and websites for major corporations and nonprofit organizations.

In 2004 Steve O'Keefe went on a road trip to interview authors all across America and Canada. Thanks to Hurricane Katrina, that road trip became a new lifestyle, leading to years on the road and 250 interviews in twenty-five cities. *Set the Page on Fire: Secrets of Successful Writers* is based on those interviews and an analysis of thousands of pitch letters, hundreds of book proposals, dozens of manuscripts, and the published works of hundreds of successful writers.

The companion website for this book is located at steve -okeefe.com. It is loaded with content and resources, including templates for the Four-Part Pitch, a book proposal template, videos from hundreds of author interviews, and other useful writing tools. You can contact the author directly at:

Steve O'Keefe
644 Greenville Ave., STE 234
Staunton, VA 24401 USA
steve-okeefe@steve-okeefe.com